**THE OFFICIAL HANDBOOK OF
ENGINEERS AND APPLIED SCIENTISTS**

TOOLIES

or
FUN, WEALTH, & ARTSY-CRAFTSIES:
What They Are and
How to Avoid Them

THE OFFICIAL HANDBOOK OF
ENGINEERS AND APPLIED SCIENTISTS

TOOLIES

or
FUN, WEALTH, & ARTSY-CRAFTSIES:
What They Are and
How to Avoid Them

by Steve Clark, P.E.

THE
DONNING COMPANY
PUBLISHERS
NORFOLK/VIRGINIA BEACH

To Dad,
without whom this book would
never have been possible—
in more ways than one.

Copyright © 1987 by Stephen Clark, P.E.

All rights reserved, including the right to reproduce this work in any form whatsoever without permission in writing from the publisher, except for brief passages in connection with a review. For information, write:
   The Donning Company/Publishers
   5659 Virginia Beach Boulevard
   Norfolk, Virginia 23502

Edited by Tony Lillis

Library of Congress Cataloging-in-Publication Data

Clark, Stephen, 1950-
   Toolies: the official handbook of engineers and applied scientists.
      1. Engineers—Anecdotes, facetiae, satire, etc.
   2. Scientists—Anecdotes, facetiae, satire, etc. I. Title.
   TA157.C49   1987   818'.5402   87-6684
   ISBN 0-89865-502-1 (pbk.)

Printed in the United States of America

CONTENTS

Acknowledgments vii

Chapter 1
Who Are The Real Toolies? 1

Chapter 2
Arts and Crafts 5

Chapter 3
The Toolie Paradox: Disciplined Inventiveness 13

Chapter 4
Tool Schools—The Toolie Top Thirty 21

Chapter 5
The Toolie Aptitude 37

Chapter 6
The Real World Paradox 51

Chapter 7
Toolie Fields 59

Chapter 8
Excitement—Living Without It 77

Chapter 9
Tool Rules 85

Chapter 10
The Metric System—Who Cares? 97

Chapter 11
Endangered Species 103

Chapter 12
They Said It Couldn't Be Done 111

Afterword 123

Index 126

Acknowledgments

A note of appreciation is owed to several people who contributed to the publication of this book.

Many thanks to the Clarks—Earl, Jerry, Linda, Bill, David, Barbara, Nancy, Jim and Blair—who time after time demonstrated a sense of humor when this toolie needed it most. Thanks also to Ron Vergakis, Mike McLaughlin, Missy Clark, Stan Brading and Steve Smith, who together give new meaning to the word "entropy."

Thanks to the University of Washington, the Folger Shakespeare Library, the Bettmann Archive, United Press International, and Culver Press, for the use of illustrations on pages 8, 9, 118, 119 and 120, respectively. Thanks to John White, in whose book *Rejection* (Addison-Wesley) many of the quotations on pages 112–114 were originally compiled. Thanks also to Richard Clark for assisting in the original photographic work for this book.

A special thanks to the artsy-craftsies, particularly Bob Friedman and Tony Lillis, at Donning Company who believed in this book—even if they were not sure that most toolies can read.

And thanks to Nancy Clark, who continuously shows me that something really can be ideal even when it's not at standard temperature and pressure.

Q. How many toolies does it take to change a light bulb?

A.
$$\left(\frac{(10x\sqrt{z^2}\overset{16.5\pi\beta^3}{-}5\beta_0^1+6z)\times|mc^2|\overset{\ln 2\alpha i}{}}{12r\int_1^{52z}\cos\phi/\sin\phi\gamma\,d\phi d\gamma + \frac{x^{1.73}\alpha\pi}{\sqrt{u^2/1-u^2}/_{\sqrt{2}}}}\right)^0 = 1.\cancel{\emptyset}3 = \underline{\underline{1}}$$

CHAPTER 1

Who Are The Real Toolies?

AS WE APPROACH the end of the twentieth century (for toolies, those are the years that start with "nineteen-"), we find ourselves in an increasingly complex technological world. In every direction we turn we see the signs of advancing technology. Man has landed on the moon, made powerful computers, explored the greatest depths of the oceans, made instantaneous worldwide communication a reality, and, except for the still uncontrollable spread of shopping malls, has discovered the cure for numerous dreaded diseases. This book is about those people most responsible for making all this possible—the Toolies.

If you are a toolie, you probably already know it. As disheartening as it may seem, you will probably remain a toolie for the rest of your life.

If you are not a toolie, there's a good chance you may think you are; even more astonishingly, you may think you want to be one. In either case, you have reason to be concerned.

CLASSIFICATIONS

There are two general classifications of toolies.

First there are the Scientists. These typically include physicists, environmentalists, biologists, chemists, mathematicians, and other people with beards.

The second general classification of toolies is the Applied Scientists. This group includes engineers, as well as programmers, draftsmen, surveyors, architects, many types of technicians, and most others who consider themselves to be dressed up while wearing at least one article of khaki clothing.

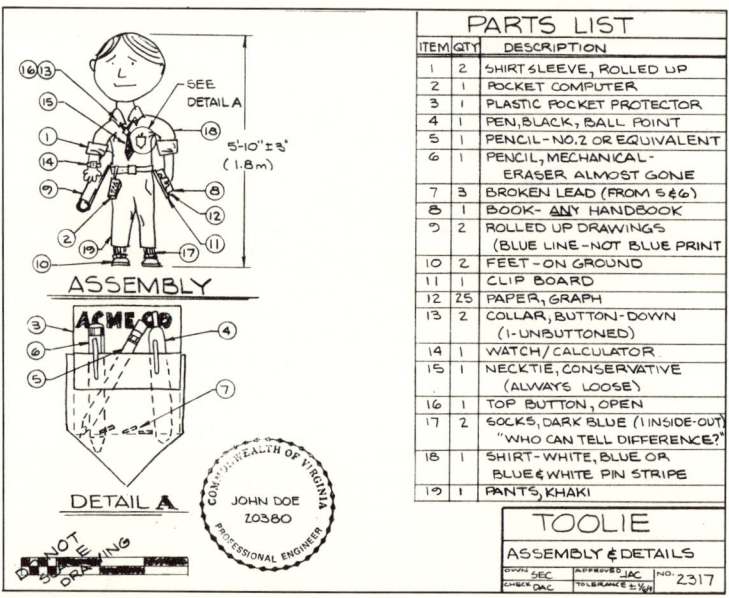

IMPOSTERS

Because of the broad public sanctions accorded toolies as the professionals responsible for mankind's most important achievements (for example, the development of the coin-operated vibrating motel bed) many toolie imposters have turned up in recent years.

The earliest known organized effort of any group of Americans to illegitimately reap the (dubious) benefits of public recognition as toolies was that of the train drivers. That's right—railroad engineers. A train driver, of course, is no more a toolie than an oil truck driver is a petroleum engineer.

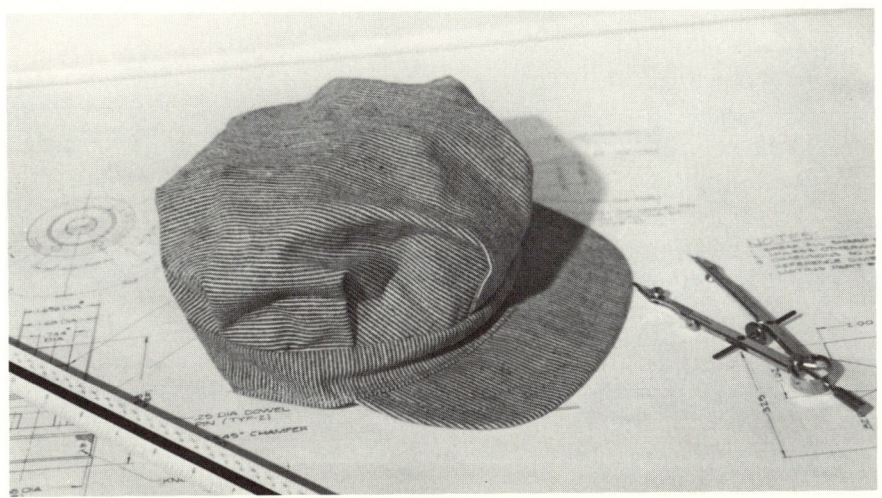

ENGINEER'S CAP?

Nonetheless, the train drivers' campaign was extraordinarily successful. Soon, people everywhere were calling train drivers railroad engineers. Then, in spite of their widespread public respect and new-found stature, it happened—they became boring.

Almost overnight, no one ever heard from them again. Just think, how many railroad engineers do you know? How many railroad engineers are known millionaires? How many railroad engineers have ever become president? Of anything?

What happened to them? Where did they all go? Authorities are not all in agreement, but the implications are as clear as an evacuated vacuum chamber.

Any professional group that tries to pass themselves off as toolies should first consider the plight of the railroad engineers. A few of those who should beware of their tenuous positions as toolie imposters are listed on the next page. (You will notice that several of those listed have already long since passed the "boredom threshold.")

TOOLIES

PEOPLE WHO WANT YOU TO THINK THEY ARE TOOLIES BUT WHO REALLY AREN'T

Psychiatrists
Psychoanalysts
Hair engineers (barbers)
Pollsters (as opposed to Surveyors)
Business Systems Analysts
Political Scientists
Social Scientists
Psychologists
Economists
Railroad Engineers (train drivers)
Sanitary Engineers (garbage collectors)
Domestic Engineers (house keepers)
Demographers
Television Weathermen
Dr. Joyce Brothers (No relationship to the Wright Brothers)
Vertical Transportation Consultants (elevator operators)
Beauty Technicians

IMPOSTERS

CHAPTER 2

Arts and Crafts

FUN AND GAMES—FORGET IT!

CONTRARY TO WHAT you've heard all your life, college is *not* all fun and games. College is not merely four years of drinking, partying, sex, ski trips, intramurals, and varsity sporting events spaced around three-month long summer vacations which are provided solely for the purpose of resting up for the next year—not, that is, unless you major in one of the liberal arts, affectionately known to toolies as "arts and crafts."

Unfortunately for you, while your artsy-craftsy friends are out having a good time, you will be staying up late nights doing physics problems, differentiating calculus problems, writing computer programs, or analyzing beam deflections. No spring vacation trips to the beaches for you. You'll be busy completing your electronic network circuit analysis or staying behind to complete two more chapters of chemistry problems.

Why, then, you may question in a rare moment of self doubt, are you studying to become a toolie rather than joining in with your

TOOLIES

SPRING VACATION

artsy-craftsy colleagues in their merrymaking? Well, for two reasons. First, you already are a toolie. Enrolling in tool school just makes it official. And second, they probably didn't invite you anyway.

ARTSY-CRAFTSIES
Give credit to your artsy-craftsy colleagues, if for no other reason (and I can't think of any) than for having the good sense not to go to tool school. After all, look where you were when they were all skiing at Mt. Killington. Although, technically speaking, you really *had* to go to tool school, the artsy-craftsy student would almost certainly have erred to have done the same, considering the wide difference between toolie and artsy-craftsy classes.

Open Book Tests
One of the first differences you will notice between toolie classes and artsy-craftsy classes is that you cannot, short of excusing yourself from

the room for a minute and running off a Xerox copy of someone else's paper, physically cheat on toolie tests.

This is because all toolie tests are Open Book tests. This has not always been the case.

In the beginning of time all colleges were artsy-craftsy schools. This was a time when large reptiles ruled the world while primitive college students wandered around aimlessly telling each other to "have a nice day." It was not a pleasant sight. Through selective breeding and natural progression the more advanced of these schools evolved into tool schools.

A carry-over from the earlier arts and crafts schools is the practice, which is still found today at many otherwise intellectual institutions, of signing a pledge on each exam paper which usually says something like:

"On my honor I have not cheated on this examination."

Although the spirit is commendable, the logic here is pure artsy-craftsy.

To avoid becoming involved with such non-self-reverse-de-incriminating rhetoric, toolies universally are permitted to use any and all available resources during all written examinations. This, as you will see soon enough, is of no help whatsoever.

Partial Credit

But perhaps the biggest academic distinction between toolie courses and artsy-craftsy courses is that in the former there are *right* and *wrong* answers; in the latter there are *right* and *acceptable* answers.

In physics, for example, when asked which is more dense, steel or cork, the only right answer is "steel." This is always the case. If you want to pass, this is what you must answer. Otherwise you fail. Long before you enrolled in tool school, a group of presumably knowledgeable toolies drew up a list of all the right answers. When your answer does not appear on that list you are considered wrong.

This attitude toward correctness is based upon a consensus opinion (at least among toolies) that, for example, a well-designed bridge should stand up. Anything else is considered a failure. Whether the bridge collapses at once, or never goes up in the first place, or just kind of sways uncontrollably when cars pass over it—each is considered a failure. Toolies are kind of funny on this point.

TACOMA NARROWS BRIDGE—No partial credit

In artsy-craftsy courses there are actually no wrong answers. So, artsy-craftsies rely on "partial credit" to get them through. In fact, partial credit accounts for 98.32 percent of all passing grades in artsy-craftsy classes.

There is, basically, only one way to fail an artsy-craftsy exam. And that's by not taking it.

For example, the works of William Shakespeare (for toolies, he was a moderately famous playwright who lived a long time ago) have been applauded for years. A true master of the English language by nearly any standard, Shakespeare is known for his unsurpassed skills of literary expression. Students of the English language strive for such an accomplished gift of communication.

Notwithstanding these accolades, 270 years after his death, English students still spend countless hours trying to decipher what Shakespeare "really" meant. So, when asked on an English exam to

TOOLIES

WILLIAM SHAKESPEARE—What did he *really* mean?

explain what *Romeo and Juliet* is about, you will pass if you say that it is a tragic story about two lovers separated by their heritage who give their lives for each other.

You will also pass if you answer that it is an introspective analysis of the cosmos as a whole, and the transcendental being from which nature, in that it is, defines itself thereto.

The second response may or may not get you an "A," depending (as is usual in artsy-craftsy courses) entirely upon the zodiacal sign and the mood of the grader at the time. But that is not the point. You will surely receive enough partial credit to pass, enabling you to get back to the tennis courts.

ARTSY-CRAFTSY CURRICULA

English is not the only liberal arts course with no wrong answers. A brief description of a few other artsy-craftsy majors is provided below.

Philosophy

This involves carefully studying the teachings of history's twelve most respected thinkers, discussing how each one totally disagrees with the thinking of the others and, upon completion of four years of such indepth evaluations, drawing no conclusions.

Psychology

Psychology is to sophomores what working on MBAs is to unemployed graduates (i.e. Psych:soph = MBA:-$grad).

If you have not chosen some other major by the end of your sophomore year, you will automatically become a psychology major. Since no one really knows anything about psychology, a lot of class time is spent looking at optical illusions and doing kinky things to pet animals.

This is pretty much what you did when you were six years old and the babysitter came to your house, but now you get college credit for it.

Sociology

Perhaps more than any other field, sociology suffers from delusions of tooliehood. Sociologists believe that, as a discipline, sociology lacks credibility unless they can convince the rest of the world that it is a science. They are, of course, correct. However, since the rest of the world knows better, their credibility is worse for the trying. No one really knows exactly what sociology is, but it's a lot like psychology, only in sociology they sit around observing groups of people instead of individual pet animals. After they graduate, sociologists then sit around trying to figure out why they majored in sociology.

Economics

Econ majors learn all the appropriate terminology necessary to "predict" yesterday's financial world occurrences. So equipped, the economist is able to explain to the uninformed masses (the rest of us) why the price of "guns" or "butter" went up or down...yesterday. At no time can an economist accurately predict what they will do tomorrow or any other time in the future.

As an economics major you will also be taught Econotalk. As in:
"Economists tell us that the increasing rate at which the decreasing speed of the rising inflations rate is steadily falling." Huh?

(Or, as toolies say: $\frac{-d^4\$}{dt^4} = C$)

TOOLIES

Economics is the field in which its most highly educated and widely respected scholar will emphatically state that the only solution to today's financial crisis is to *raise* taxes while at the same time its second most respected and equally well-qualified representative says, just as emphatically, that the only valid solution to today's financial crisis is to *lower* taxes. Obviously both should get partial credit.

Graduate Work

If after four years of artsy-craftsy partying you failed to ingratiate yourself to at least one fellow partier whose father could get you a high-paying job after graduation (surely nothing you learned in arts and crafts class is of any use in the nine-to-five world) there is always graduate school.

For the more ambitious, there are always law and medical schools. But they're both so, shall we say, goal-oriented.

At the other end of the scale is the option to get a masters in your undergraduate major. This option is a good idea for artsy-craftsies with zero imagination. Hence, there are a lot of artsy-craftsies doing just that.

With a masters degree in arts and crafts the only thing you will be vocationally competent to do for the rest of your life is teach. But since you will be overqualified* to teach in elementary or high school, you will be obliged to continue on and get a doctorate in some narrow and obscure field so that you can teach on the college level. The most attractive aspect of this option is that it tacks on another couple of years of college, giving you yet another opportunity to ingratiate yourself to someone with corporate ties.

Imbeeay

The direction preferred by most artsy-craftsy graduates is the masters in business administration ("imbeeay") route. By taking just one introductory accounting class at any school in the country, you will indefinitely be allowed to classify your status as "working on my

---

* "Overqualified" is undeniably the ultimate artsy-craftsy misnomer.

TOOLIES

imbeeay." Informal polls suggest that at any given time at least nine out of ten artsy-craftsy graduates consider themselves to be working on their imbeeays.

Not only does this option sound impressive, but one course is good for a lifetime and it completely justifies either why you're not employed, why you're employed where you are, or anything else that you think needs explaining. As in, "I was thinking of taking a few weeks off and sailing to the islands, but I'm busy working on my imbeeay." Or, "I'm just driving this taxi for a few years until I get my imbeeay."

CHAPTER 3

The Toolie Paradox: Disciplined Inventiveness

TO BE SURE, the years spent in college are always important. But for toolies, the significance of the college experience is immeasurable. Colleges and universities offering studies to toolies (Tool Schools) are burdened with a most important task, one which is unparalleled in the halls of academia.

Prior to enrolling in college, toolies are characterized by their inventive minds, their resolution of seemingly unsolvable tasks, their innovative spirits, their novel and resourceful approach to unusual problems, and their unmatched curiosity for exploring real and theoretical frontiers. If there ever were a group of leading-edge, trend-setting individuals, it is surely the pre-college toolies.

It is, then, the immense responsibility of our colleges and universities to change this congregation of potential world-shapers into the single most boring group of look-alike, think-alike individuals this side of the Pro Golfers' Tour. And, as you have probably noticed, it is a responsibility they do not take lightly. Since it is an extremely ambitious goal to accomplish this metamorphosis in just four short years, many universities have found it necessary to offer their toolie students five-year programs and, just to make sure, graduate studies.

If you receive a graduate degree as a toolie you may notice that you have obtained a new insight into, or a certain knack for, dullness. (Surely, your associates will have noticed as much about you.) If such is the case, you will want to give serious consideration to the possibility of becoming a Toolie Professor. As a toolie professor you too can teach legions of young innovators the virtues of similartude. But being a toolie professor is not nearly so easy as you may think. The National Toolie Accreditation Board maintains an extremely close watch over toolie instructors to ensure that they strictly adhere to the requirements of the ToolProf's Code.

The ToolProf's Code is the legislative standard which requires that at least one out of every four toolie test questions be based on either a 3-4-5 or 30°-60°-90° triangle. And there's also Section 12.6 of the code, for example, which demands that the expression "free body diagram" be used in every toolie class—regardless of whether or not it is even remotely applicable.

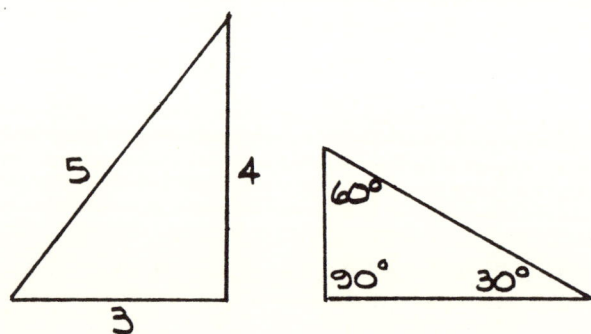

Though such requirements are difficult to adjust to at first, toolie professors generally find that with practice they can smoothly plug overworked expressions like these into virtually every conversation. Of course, when nobody listens to you, you *can* pretty well say anything that you want.

THE TOOLIE CURRICULUM

Some lowlifes believe that the toolie curriculum leads to a limited amount of knowledge, by a limited group of people, who concentrate on extremely limited fields of study. It is only fair to note that such a belief is usually espoused by people with an arts and crafts education which, arguably, constitutes a contradiction of terms in itself.

It is widely recognized that the toolie curriculum is based upon in-depth studies of the Universal Laws of Nature. But because these laws are studied in such great depth and in classes with such esoteric sounding titles (i.e. Advanced Partial Differential Equations of Classical Three-Dimensional Newtonian Physics, 201—Excuuuse me!), the "universal" applications and significance of these courses are understandably overlooked and rarely appreciated by outsiders.

It is also widely recognized that the toolie curriculum is primarily made up of courses that specifically address the technical skills and knowledge necessary to become productive professionals in the various toolie fields. Electrical engineers learn about electricity. Mechanical engineers learn about mechanics. And an attempt is made to teach civil engineers how to act civilized.

But if you can survive a toolie education, you will also indirectly pick up many other skills. And in this regard, the toolie education may actually be the most liberal education of all.

For example, by the time you graduate from tool school you will have learned enough math to have been an *accounting* major with one hand tied behind your back, or to have majored in *economics* with your eyes closed—(which, in fact, may well be the norm).

Without taking the first *education* course, you will learn how to teach people who you will never even meet how to do things that no one before you has ever contemplated.

Your precise use of the English language, although less flourished and verbose, will nonetheless rival or surpass the invented diction of the average *journalism* or *English* major in its ability to communicate rational concepts.

In addition to mastering the use of mathematics (the "language of science," we are told), you will become highly skilled in at least one, but probably two or three, highly complex and notoriously unforgiving computer languages, each of which you will use daily in

TOOLIES

nearly all of your toolie courses. This curriculum by itself is nearly equivalent to a minor in a *foreign language*.

You will have learned volumes about the mathematics of sampling techniques and statistics, and will develop an awareness of action-response correlation surpassing that which forms the essence of most *psychology* curricula.

You will not only methodically and intensively investigate and study past phenomena (some of which may even predate the origin of the earth itself) but you will in nearly every case go your *history* colleagues one better by regularly predicting future events based on such studies.

You will have developed a lifelong expertise in the art of objective observation of both laboratory and "real world" environments that should be the envy of all *sociology* majors.

You will learn to use an exactness of speech, an affinity for details, and an appreciation for logical progression of events which will make you a strong candidate for *law* school in the event you should decide to change from the study of natural laws to statutory laws.

You will achieve an ability to think and develop abstract concepts to a degree that *philosophy* majors only dream. Your studies in logic and inductive and deductive reasoning will be so complete as to make similar studies taken up by these philosophy majors seem second nature to you.

You will devleop skills enabling you to transform abstract thoughts into state-of-the-art masterpieces, the value and striking beauty against which the efforts of many an *art* major turns pale.

All the while, it is not unlikely that, during your four or more years in tool school, you will take "elective" courses in several liberal arts programs, giving you a "healthy" dose of psych, econ, and business to complement your already extensive toolie education.

During your four or more years of formal toolie education you will not, alas, learn to sing. (To be honest, most toolies sing like frogs. And you're no exception).

In spite of all this apparently well-rounded education, you will nonetheless have to endure many years of disparaging remarks from artsy-craftsies who frequently imply, and often offer flat out discourses on the one-sided shallowness of the uncompromising and ill-informed toolie.

If you learn anything at all during your four years at tool school, you will most certainly learn how to stoically endure such misguided sentiments.

THE TOOLIE STUDENT

Edgar Pimpleton
Nickname: "Univac"
Mechanical Engineering
Won regional engineering society competition for technical paper titled "Infinite Element Analysis of Diatonic Membranes Using the Pimpleton Wave Approximation Method of Elasticity;" License tags: "ENGR;" Student member ASME, NSPE, ASHRAE; Vice-President, "Gears 'N Sprockets" Club; Member, Future Engineers of America.
SAT's: Math 790, Verbal 600

UNIVAC

Tchu San Li
Nickname: "Tu-Li"
Double major. Electrical Engineering/Mathematics
Has memorized value of Pi to 18 digits; Student member AIEE, ASSE, IEEE; after graduation will return to Orient to undermine American technology; Dormitory table tennis champion.
SAT's (Special Foreign Student exchange waiver)

TU-LI

TOOLIES

Frederick George Copeland
Nickname: "Fred"
FRED
Civil Engineering (started in mechanical, switched major in junior year)
Third place finish annual engineering school egg drop contest; "Took engineering to avoid foreign language requirement;" Owns a set of golf clubs but never actually uses them; Student member AAA (American Automobile Association); Worked as draftsman during summer vacation.
SAT's: Math 660, Verbal 420

Mary Clark Chadwick
Nickname: "MC^2", "Bytes"
MC^2
Computer Science
Student member AAAS, AICE, ASCE; Work/study program—works at computer center two nights per week; First in class to have job lined up after graduation; Intramural volleyball, hockey. "Curve Buster," *always* turns in homework on time; never uses script when writing—always prints.
SAT's: Math 560, Verbal 650

TOOLIES

17 SUBJECTS THAT ALL TOOLIES STUDY BUT NEVER USE (in the Real World)

1. Avogadro's number
2. Mohr's circle
3. Matrices
4. Partial Differential Equations
5. Heizenberg Uncertainty Principle
6. Calculus
7. The Quadratic Equation
8. Imaginary numbers
9. Hyperbolic anything
10. Laplace (or anybody else's) Transformations
11. Entropy
12. Schroedinger Wave Equation
13. g_c
14. The limit of anything as it approaches zero
15. Sets and subsets
16. Index of Refraction
17. Dot and Cross Products (*especially* Dot Products)

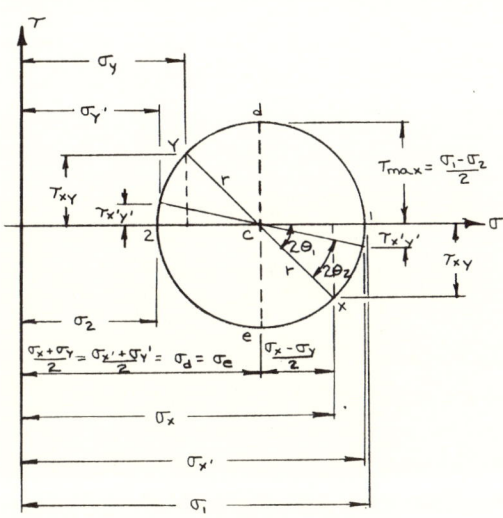

MOHR'S CIRCLE

CHAPTER 4

Tool Schools— The Toolie Top Thirty

OF THE OVER fifteen hundred four-year colleges and universities in the United States, some three hundred offer curricula leading to bachelor's degrees in being a toolie. These are, by definition, the three hundred best schools in the land. But of this elite group of institutions—which themselves represent the top 20 pecent of American institutions of higher learning—which ones are truly the top schools? To many, this may seem a little like asking which of a group of expecting women is the most pregnant. This skepticism is understandable. Skepticism is always understandable. Metaphorically speaking, the edge here is given to those carrying quintuplets.

The Toolie Top Thirty, below, lists the best of the best. The institutions are divided into two groups. The first are the classic tool schools—those which, for all intents and purposes, cater specifically to toolies or which are most widely known for their toolie curricula.

The second group includes institutions not generally recognized as tool schools, but which, in addition to their outstanding liberal arts curricula, also offer the best toolie programs. Graduates of these universities not only have experienced the best of toolie educations, but have also been exposed to life with liberal arts students from which actual real world occurrences can be, if not experienced, at least observed.

Although specific criteria for selection to this list is quite involved, a good rule of thumb is that six-week computer programming schools and those schools whose primary means of gaining public exposure comes from advertisements on the inside of matchbook covers, in general, did not fare too well on this list. And although in each case the "whole" university was considered, information such as class rankings and SAT's given usually only apply to the tool students.

In addition to those schools cited below, special recognition should also be given to Purdue University, University of Michigan, New Jersey Tech, Penn State, and North Carolina State. An impressive one out of every nine toolies in the entire United States earns a degree from one of these five institutions. By sheer numbers alone—and for most toolie analyses what else is there?—these would have to be considered five of the premier tool schools in the country.

THE TOOLIE TOP THIRTY
EXCELLENT TOOL SCHOOLS
THAT LOOK LIKE EXCELLENT
TOOL SCHOOLS

1. MIT
2. Cal Tech
3. Rensselaer
4. Harvey Mudd
5. Rose-Hulman
6. Rice
7. Case-Western
8. Carnegie-Mellon
9. Worchester Tech
10. Lehigh
11. Union College
12. Georgia Tech
13. Virginia Tech
14. Clarkson
15. Cooper Union

TOOLIES

EXCELLENT TOOL SCHOOLS
THAT LOOK LIKE EXCELLENT
ALL-AROUND SCHOOLS
1. Cornell
2. Duke
3. Princeton
4. Stanford
5. Johns Hopkins
6. Columbia
7. Northwestern
8. Pennsylvania
9. Virginia
10. Washington (Mo.)
11. Notre Dame
12. University of California, Berkley
13. Tufts
14. Lafayette
15. Illinois (Urbanna)

EXCELLENT TOOL SCHOOLS THAT LOOK LIKE EXCELLENT TOOL SCHOOLS

1. MASSACHUSETTS INSTITUTE OF TECHNOLOGY
   Cambridge, Massachusetts
   Private, Founded 1861

So many people refer to this school as simply MIT that almost no one knows that it is located in Massachusetts. However, those that do will tell you that the entire intellectual world revolves around the Cambridge-Boston area. (These people, of course, tend to be either the area's inhabitants or their brainwashed relatives). MIT is the nation's most distinguished school of engineering and science. Over 98 percent of MIT's students graduated in the top fifth of their high school class and no one in school got even close to scoring as low as 600 on the math SAT. Even though some 80 percent of its classes are electives, academic pressures are considered to be all but overwhelming at MIT.

2. CALIFORNIA INSTITUTE OF TECHNOLOGY
   Pasadena, California
   Private, Founded 1891

Although Cal Tech may be the most prestigious science and engineering school in the country, it is (at best) the second most well

TOOLIES

known edifice in Pasadena. This turns out to be an invaluable educational experience which will prove to be useful in the future to Tech toolies in explaining, for example, why brainless athletes annually pay more in taxes than toolies receive in gross income. To be sure, there is not a more able student body in the United States, and there is not one its equal within 2500 miles. Like MIT, 98 percent of Cal Tech's students graduated in the top fifth of their high school class, and only two students in one hundred score below 700 on the math SAT. Although there are no set requirements and each student helps devise his own curriculum, the dropout rate at Cal Tech is fairly high. (Twenty-eight percent drop out, which is very high for an institution that screens its applicants so thoroughly).

3. RENSSELAER POLYTECHNIC INSTITUTE
Troy, New York
Private, Founded 1824

RPI is the oldest tool school in the United States, and it has always been one of the very best. Three quarters of RPI's students graduate in the top fifth of their high school class, and 92 percent score over 600 on the math SAT. Being 150 miles north of New York City, Rensselaer toolies are adequately removed from any unnecessary infusion of culture.

4. HARVEY MUDD COLLEGE
Claremont, California
Private, Founded 1955

Although it's a relatively new school, Harvey Mudd is one of the most selective institutions in the country and has a highly educated student body. HMC is the member of the Claremont College system that specializes in engineering, math, and physical science. One-third of all undergraduate courses are in the humanities, the most of any tool school in the country. With only about five hundred students, Harvey Mudd is able to provide financial aid to any who are qualified and in need. However, qualifying is pretty tough here. Ninety-one percent graduated in the top fifth of their high school class, and only about one student per class scores below 600 on the math SAT.

5. ROSE-HULMAN INSTITUTE OF TECHNOLOGY
Terre Haute, Indiana
Private, Founded 1874

Formerly Rose Polytechnic Institute, R-HIT is probably the best unknown tool school in the United States. This is your basic excellent tool school! The faculty is generally oriented toward teaching (rather than research), 91 percent of its students graduated in the top fifth of their high school class, and 85 percent score over 600 on the math SAT. However, if you're looking for a normal social life (which you shouldn't be) you may want to look elsewhere. Rose is not coed.

6. RICE UNIVERSITY
Houston, Texas
Private, Founded 1891

Rice is far and away the outstanding academic institution of a region that has produced few (or no) other first rank universities. One fifth of Rice's students are National Merit scholars. Although not strictly a tool school, one-third of Rice's students do receive engineering degrees. Toolies here have the option of a five-year program and 95 percent who enter as freshmen actually graduate, which is admirably high. Eighty percent graduate in the top fifth of their high school class and 88 percent score over 600 on the math SAT.

7. CASE WESTERN RESERVE UNIVERSITY
Cleveland, Ohio
Private, Founded 1826

Case Western was formed by the recent merger of Case Institute of Technology (tool school) and Western Reserve (arts and crafts school). In spite of administrative efforts to the contrary, it is still possible for tool school students to go through four years without encountering any artsy-craftsies. Nonetheless, one in three CW toolies drop out before graduation. For the tool school, 86 percent graduate in the top fifth of their high school class, and 90 percent score over 600 on the math SAT.

TOOLIES

8. CARNEGIE-MELLON UNIVERSITY
   Pittsburgh, Pennsylvania
   Private, Founded 1900

Carnegie-Mellon was formed by the merger of Carnegie Institute of Technology and the Mellon Institute. Fifteen percent of its graduates go on to medical or law schools, but 39 percent earn engineering, math, or science degrees. Eighty-seven percent graduate in the top fifth of their high school class and 84 percent score over 600 on the math SAT. Though located in industrial Pittsburgh, students here employ decidely agrarian terms to distinguish between toolies and artsy-craftsies. The former are called "veggies;" the latter are called (ahem) "fruits."

9. WORCHESTER POLYTECHNIC INSTITUTE
   Worchester, Massachusetts
   Private, Founded 1865

Worchester (pronounced "wooster") is the third oldest independent tool school in the United States. Students here seem to be overwhelmingly concerned with occupational and professional goals—all those, that is, except for the nearly 40 percent who never graduate (perhaps due to too many trips to nearby Boston, which is only fifty miles away). The average senior has twelve company interviews. Eighty percent graduate in the top fifth of their high school class. Seventy percent score over 600 on the math SAT.

10. LEHIGH UNIVERSITY
    Bethlehem, Pennsylvania
    Private, Founded 1865

Lehigh is a very well known undergraduate engineering college whose graduates tend to be more broadly educated than graduates of many other tool schools. Twenty-one percent go to medical or law schools. Bethlehem is an industrial city some sixty miles away from any identifiable form of culture. But unlike most other tool schools, Lehigh is so widely known as a party school that outsiders actually *come to* it on the weekends. Nicknamed the "Engineers," you just *know* visiting teams are intimidated to play here. Seventy percent graduate in the top fifth of their high school class and 72 percent score over 600 on the math SAT.

11. UNION COLLEGE
    Schenectady, New York
    Private, Founded 1795

Union College, located near the state's capital of Albany, is justifiably proud that in 1845 it was the nation's first liberal arts college that had the good sense to introduce an engineering program. This move, however academically admirable it may be, probably helps account for why few people outside of New York are familiar with Union College. Three quarters of UC's students are from New York. Eighty-three percent of UC's very capable student body graduate in the top fifth of their high school class and 67 percent score over 600 on the math SAT.

12. GEORGIA INSTITUTE OF TECHNOLOGY
    Atlanta, Georgia
    State, Founded 1885

Georgia Tech is one of the most prestigious engineering schools in the South, and has the largest undergraduate toolie student body of any tool school in the United States. With some nine thousand toolies all in the same place, it takes all Atlanta can offer to maintain its reputation as one of the most exciting cities in America. The student-to-teacher ratio here is rather high, but students can take five years to graduate, significantly increasing the odds over four year students of eventually running into a teacher. Seventy-eight percent graduate in the top fifth of their high school class and 56 percent score over 600 on the math SAT.

13. VIRGINIA POLYTECHNIC INSTITUTE
    AND STATE UNIVERSITY
    Blacksburg, Virginia
    State, Founded 1872

Quite the opposite of, say, Colorado School of Mines, VPI & SU reigns as the most pretentiously named tool school in the United

TOOLIES

States, (though Cooper Union for the Advancement of Science & Art better watch out). It seems that the schools of home economics, agriculture, and education felt offended that Virginia Tech had developed such a fine reputation as "just" a tool school, so a few years back they added "and State University" to their name—as though that made any difference. Virginia Tech is rapidly becoming one of the country's most selective tool schools. Seventy-eight percent graduate in the top fifth of their high school class and 63 percent score over 600 on the math SAT.

14. CLARKSON INSTITUTE OF TECHNOLOGY
    Potsdam, New York
    Private, Founded 1896

Clarkson is located in a small town (pop. 10,000) about 140 miles north of Syracuse, New York. If you haven't checked lately, Syracuse is only about a long three-wood (that's golf talk) from the North Pole. For those who can weather it, Clarkson is a quiet school with a strict engineering curriculum. About 65 percent graduate in the top fifth of their high school class, and 67 percent score over 600 on the math SAT.

15. COOPER UNION FOR THE ADVANCEMENT
    OF SCIENCE AND ART
    New York City
    Private, Founded 1859

Hidden in Greenwich Village in New York City, Cooper Union is about the last place one might expect to find one of the best tool schools in the land. Once a tuition free college, CU now runs an incredibly low three hundred dollars (or so) fee a year. The school fields no intercollegiate teams, so there's plenty of time available for hitting the books. Or for reading them if you prefer. Ninety-eight percent graduate in the top fifth of their high school class and 98 percent score over 600 on the math SAT.

TOOLIES

EXCELLENT TOOL SCHOOLS THAT LOOK LIKE EXCELLENT ALL-AROUND SCHOOLS

1. CORNELL UNIVERSITY
Ithaca, New York
Private, Founded 1865

Cornell is truly one of the nation's finest all around universities. Of Cornell's several schools, its engineering school is reported to offer the most intense academic pressures. (This report, of course, comes most frequently from Cornell's toolies.) Cornell has more buildings (four hundred) than a lot of schools have computer terminals. Cornell is one of four Ivy League schools included in the top ten all-around tool schools. Eighteen percent of Cornell's students are engineering students. Ninety percent of students graduate in the top fifth of their high school class and about 94 percent score over 600 on the math SAT. Though surrounded by a striking campus, Cornell toolies are rarely distracted from their studies, as the four seasons (rain, drizzle, slush, and snow) offer little incentive to go outdoors.

2. DUKE UNIVERSITY
Durham, North Carolina
Private (with United Methodist ties), Founded 1838

Duke is one of only a few Southern universities that is also a major national institution. Durham is located in one corner of what North Carolinians refer to as the "Research Triangle." (North Carolina State University in Raleigh and University of North Carolina in Chapel Hill—both excellent tool schools—are located at the other two corners of the triangle). Duke has an outstanding tool school with 94 percent of its students having graduated in the top fifth of their high school class, and 96 percent scoring over 600 on the math SAT. Even though every other student you run into seems to be in pre-med, Duke is nonetheless one of the best places in the country to get a toolie education.

TOOLIES

3. PRINCETON UNIVERSITY
   Princeton, New Jersey
   Private, Founded 1746

With well over two hundred years of experience to draw upon, Princeton is knee deep in tradition. To its credit, Princeton has held onto many old values, such as having its senior faculty still teach undergraduate classes, a practice which has been slowly phased out in many other universities. Twenty-one percent of its students are in architecture and engineering and another 17 percent in math and sciences. Princeton is roughly equidistant between New York City and Philadelphia, providing both adequate opportunity as well as adequate buffer from the cultural experiences of each. Ninety percent graduate in the top fifth of their high school classes, and 77 percent score over 600 on the math SAT.

4. STANFORD UNIVERSITY
   Palo Alto, California
   Private, Founded 1885

Stanford is probably the most prestigious university in the nation...that is not located on the East Coast. Stanford has one of the nation's highest teacher-to-student ratios for a university of its size (1 to 10). About half of Stanford's students major in engineering, mathematics, or science. Of those, 94 percent graduate in the top fifth of their high school class, and 77 percent score over 600 on the math SAT.

5. JOHNS HOPKINS UNIVERSITY
   Baltimore, Maryland
   Private, Founded 1876

Johns Hopkins is a non-denominational school, unless you count devout lacrosse zealots, who account for about 96 percent of the student body. JHU places strong emphasis on graduate education. Its medical school, for example, is one of the most distinguished in the nation. Less well-known, but infinitely more important, is the fact that Johns Hopkins' student body is made up of 20 percent engineering and 45 percent math and science majors. For the toolies at JHU, 88 percent graduate in the top fifth of their high school class and 84 percent score over 600 on their math SAT.

6. COLUMBIA UNIVERSITY (School of Engineering
   & Applied Science)
   New York, New York
   Private, Founded 1810

Everybody, including toolies, at Columbia is required to take two years of strong liberal arts study before getting fully into their (far more important) toolie studies. Between the liberal arts classes and all of the distractions of living in Manhattan, Columbia toolies are hard pressed to avoid being overwhelmed by all this culture—but it's worth a try. Eighty-nine percent graduate in the top fifth of their high school class and 88 percent score over 600 on the math SAT.

7. NORTHWESTERN UNIVERSITY
   Evanston, Illinois
   Private, Founded 1851

Northwestern is a highly selective university located on the shores of Lake Michigan in the suburbs of Chicago. Toolies at Northwestern make up about 9 percent of the entire student body, with 90 percent graduating in the top fifth of their high school class and 87 percent scoring over 600 on the math SAT. Ninety percent of Northwestern's graduates are accepted for medical, dental, or law schools.

8. UNIVERSITY OF PENNSYLVANIA
   Philadelphia, Pennsylvania
   Private, Founded 1740

Founded by the famous eighteenth century toolie Ben Franklin, Penn is the oldest university in the Toolie Top Thirty. This was the first institution of higher learning to offer subjects such as applied mathematics and the sciences, and thus is considered the nation's first "true" university. (Toolies will argue that if math and science aren't offered then it couldn't possibly have been "higher learning" in the first place). Penn's library is the largest open-stack library in an

American university, having over three million volumes and forty-six thousand items.

9. UNIVERSITY OF VIRGINIA
    Charlottesville, Virginia
    State, Founded 1819

UVA is the most prestigious public university in the nation. Virginia's nationally represented student body may receive about the best education per dollar tuition of any major university. But although 89 percent graduate in the top fifth of their high school class and 89 percent score over 600 on the math SAT, UVA toolies are handicapped by the pervasive rumor that anything that was ever worth inventing or discovering was done long ago by the school's founder and architect, Thomas Jefferson.

10. WASHINGTON UNIVERSITY
    St. Louis, Missouri
    Private, Founded 1853

A very good all-around university, Washington's toolie students are both its most numerous (16 percent of the student body) and its most capable (87 percent graduate in the top fifth of their high school class and 87 percent score over 600 on the math SAT). Like several of the top tool schools, there are a lot of future doctors running around at this midwestern university, but, for the most part, they're harmless.

11. UNIVERSITY OF NOTRE DAME
    South Bend, Indiana
    Private (with Catholic ties), Founded 1842

The major interest here for the 91 percent of the students who are not toolies is football. Once that is noted, however, Notre Dame stands as an excellent academic institution. All toolies here are required to take the same common courses during freshman year, but overall elective courses account for nearly 70 pecent of UND classes. Roughly 88 percent graduate in the top fifth of their high school class and 74 percent score over 600 on the math SAT.

TOOLIES

12. UNIVERSITY OF CALIFORNIA AT BERKLEY
Berkley, California (where else?)
State, Founded 1868

UC Berkley is the largest (twenty-nine thousand graduate and undergraduate) and most prestigious of the nine University of California campuses. Eleven percent of Berkley's students are toolies and the remaining 89 percent are political activists. A high student-to-faculty ratio at this huge school results in minimal contact between faculty and students. This helps prepare Berkley toolies for their professional roles mired in anonymity. Berkley has earned most of its outstanding reputation from its research and graduate programs. Though only a small part of this trickles down to undergraduates, it still results in an excellent toolie education.

13. TUFTS UNIVERSITY
Medford, Massachusetts
Private, Founded 1852

The third Massachusetts school in the Toolie Top Thirty, Tufts has about 4500 undergraduate students, 18 percent of which earn engineering degrees. Tufts has long been regarded as a very attractive haven for Ivy League also-rans. Only 1 percent of the freshman class drops out. Seventy-eight percent of Tufts' students graduate in the top fifth of their high school class and 72 percent score over 600 on the math SAT.

14. LAFAYETTE COLLEGE
Easton, Pennsylvania
Private, Founded 1826

Lafayette is a small undergradute liberal arts school (two thousand students) which acts in many ways like a classic tool school. Lafayette's tool school is over one hundred years old. Twenty-seven percent of Lafayette's students graduate from its very strong engineering/technical program. Most of Lafayette's students, even its artsy-craftsies, are primarily interested in preparing for their future jobs or graduate school. Eighty-six percent graduate in the top fifth of their high school class and 69 percent score over 600 on the math SAT.

TOOLIES

15. UNIVERSITY OF ILLINOIS (Urbanna campus)
    Urbanna, Illinois
    State, Founded 1867

University of Illinois has more toolie graduates than any other school in the Toolie Top Thirty and its academic library is also the largest in the Toolie Top Thirty. Illinois is a very selective and very large school (over thirty-three thousand students) whose academic pressures are described as only moderately intense, but from which less than two-thirds of its entering freshmen ever earn degrees. Not a big drawing card to out-of-staters, virtually all Illinois toolies (97 percent) come from the state of Illinois. Illinois' tool school is one of its many strong points, and about one in seven Illini are toolies. Of these, 84 percent graduate in the top fifth of their high school class.

AUTHOR'S NOTE:

FOR THOSE WHO AGREE with the data given in this list, it should be of interest that absolutely every conceivable qualitative and quantitative aspect (and their respective precise influence on the overall quality) of the listed colleges and universities has been methodically and accurately accounted for in the derivation of this list. I am proud to acknowledge that the Toolie Top Thirty is the very first list of its kind to have taken *every* such element into consideration.

FOR THOSE WHO DISAGREE with the data given in this list, your objection is well taken. The information used in compiling this list was both biased and inexcusably out-of-date. Schools for which unjustifiably low rankings are shown were in most instances not given proper credit in those areas where they are actually the strongest. It would be fair for you to assume that if a survey were taken today to update data on these slighted schools, in *every* instance the ranking of the slighted institutions would be not only higher, but *significantly* higher. I apologize for these oversights.

TOOLIES

SEVEN SUBJECTS THAT AREN'T WHAT THEY SAY THEY ARE

1. "Elementary" Particle Physics
2. "Fundamental" Relativity
3. "Basic" Quantum Mechanics
4. "Ordinary" Differential Equations
5. "Determinate" Structures
6. "Finite" Systems Analysis
7. "Advanced" Psychology

CHAPTER 5

The Toolie Aptitude

IF YOU ARE a toolie, the odds are (P(Toolie)/P(Not a Toolie) > 1.0) that you were born a toolie. In fact, there is a very strong chance that one of your parents is at least a latent, if not a registered, toolie. This may be stated because a positive hereditary correlation has been demonstrated between toolie-bearing adults and a general inability of those adults to wear plaid clothing.

As though that were not enough proof, a hereditary link between toolies was recently verified during studies conducted in the remotest islands of the Southeast Pacific, in which entire tribes were found to have existed without any known toolies for hundreds of generations.

(Simultaneous studies have also shown that these same people live in straw houses set on the edges of smoldering volcanoes, have an average life span of 18.6 years, subsist on a diet of only tree bark and prunes, and have no plumbing facilities whatsoever).

NO PLAID

TOOLETS

Usually the toolie aptitude is first evident in babies and young children, or Toolets. The Surgeon General has recommended that parents of young children be on the lookout for the Early Warning Signs for toolets. These signs include such seemingly "normal" behavior as being good with building blocks (civil/structural); throwing objects across the room (aerospace); playing in dirt (civil); writing on walls (drafting); pouring contents (mostly) from one container to another and (mostly) back again (chemical/fluid dynamics); spinning tops with utter fascination (mechanical/gyrophysics); playing with television and radio dials (computers); or incessantly turning off and on light switches (electrical). If such seemingly innocuous behavior is left unchecked, permanent and irreversible consequences (yes, an increase in entropy) can result.

Many times such toolie traits are not as overt as these, and other, more direct, methods must be used to isolate the true toolie aptitude. The following Toolie Aptitude Test is provided as a guide for making such a determination.

CAUTION: This test is only to be used as a guide in helping to determine the presence of latent toolie aptitude. If this test proves positive, consult your physician immediately.

TOOLIES

TOOLET

TOOLIE APTITUDE TEST

1. In the figure below, which direction will pulley B turn if handle A is turned in the direction shown?
a) Direction 1
b) Direction 2
c) What's a pulley?
d) Cannot be determined without knowing speed of pulley A.
e) Just turn the goddamn thing and see which way it turns.
f) Most likely the handle stem will break and pulley B will not turn at all.

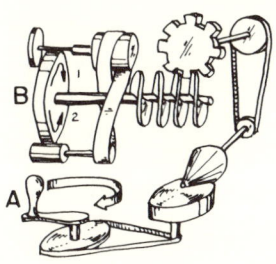

ANSWER: a) or b), of course, are *not* the correct answers, and if you thought they were, you might need to get your eyes checked. Answer c) is a classic artsy-craftsy answer. Answer d) is a classic answer from an artsy-craftsy who is trying to act like a toolie. Real toolies will always pick e) or f).

2. When attending an elaborate wedding ceremony, you most likely sit quietly in awe of...
    a) the bride
    b) the bride's gown
    c) What's an awe?
    d) the intricate detail and symmetry of the church's design

ANSWER: Part credit for answering a), no credit for answering b) or c). The obvious toolie choice is d).

3. When thumbing through a copy of *Scientific American* magazine, you would most likely open to...
    a) the first page. You always start at the beginning.
    b) the last page. You like to know where the author's going before spending your time reading his work.
    c) any page with pictures.
    d) None of the above. You don't have time to thumb through *Scientific American* because you're too busy with your encounter group sessions.

ANSWER: Only answer d) can be classified as an artsy-craftsy answer. If you picked answer d), you don't even need to go to the next question. Just go. Trust me, you are *not* toolie material.

4. Which of the following books can be found in your home, office, or dorm room?
    a) Any Haliday and Resnick physics book
    b) Any Shaums outline
    c) *Mark's Handbook of Mechanical Engineering*
    d) *CRC Handbook of Math Tables*
    e) *Machinery's Handbook*
    f) Hell, I can't find *anything* in my office.

TOOLIES

ANSWER: Score one point for each book checked. Score one extra point for each book checked that you have actually read. Subtract two points if you have actually read *all the way through* any of these books. Score one extra point if you checked c) and you don't think that you're a mechanical engineer. Add twenty points if f) was the only answer you checked. Subtract twenty points if this answer is too complicated for you to understand.

5. Upon reaching the top floor of an elegant high rise office building, you are most likely...
    a) at your office.
    b) at your home.
    c) on the wrong floor, having pushed the wrong number on the elevator.
    d) riddled with anxiety because the building was constructed by builders with eighth grade educations.

ANSWER: a) not likely, but no demerits for choosing this answer. Answer b) is definitely wrong. A toolie could hardly afford such a luxury. Answer c) is wrong because toolies do not push wrong numbers. Answer d) is the toolie answer.

6. On your first trip to St. Louis, and upon arriving at the six hundred foot high Gateway Arch, you will most likely...
   a) be impressed with this engineering marvel.
   b) ascend to its top and view the splendor of the panoramic vista.
   c) stay on the ground, suspecting that the construction contract for the Arch went to the lowest bidder.
   d) dwell on the historical significance of the landmark.

   ANSWER: Answer c) is the most common toolie response. Answer a) is too obvious, but ok. Answers b) and d) are disgusting and wrong, respectively—especially if you used those exact words.

7. Look closely at the picture of the beautiful model below. Which of the following thoughts first enter your mind?
   a) Free Body diagram
   b) Cantilever structures
   c) Significant figures
   d) French curves
   e) None of of the above

   ANSWER: Only answer e) is an artsy-craftsy answer.

8. You would most likely wear a pair of red and green plaid pants...
    a) at Christmas time only.
    b) with a conservative, solid white Oxford button-down collared shirt.
    c) with a matching plaid sport coat.
    d) only to your own execution.
    e) never.

ANSWER: The correct answer is e). Answer a), though, can be excused as an incorrect answer given without proper consideration. Answer b), however, cannot be excused because it is an incorrect answer *with* proper consideration. If you answered c), go to the explanation for answer 3d above. Even answer d) is not a proper toolie response. Why would you want to borrow some artsy-craftsy's pants just for your execution?

(For questions 9-16, examinee (that's the person who is taking the exam) is to define the following words, before looking at the choice answers. Use graphic scale).

9. Define "Jiggle"
    a) motion of buxom women's breasts seen at beginning of many prime time television programs
    b) the sound of money in your pocket
    c) initial remedial action used to stop water from running

ANSWER: b) is correct only if this represents your weekly allowance. Otherwise, c) is the correct answer.

10. Define "Specs"
    a) small particles or dots
    b) eyeglasses
    c) details
    d) suspicion (as in, "He 'specs it's 'bout 6.9 meters long.")

ANSWER: Answer c) is correct. "Specs" is short for specifications.

TOOLIES

11. Define a "Common Log"
    a) a diary, usually kept at sea
    b) a standard six-inch diameter, two-foot long piece of fire wood
    c) the power to which ten is raised to produce a given number
    d) a vulgar, disgusting piece of lumber

    ANSWER: Answer c) is correct. Artsy-craftsies normally say d).

12. Define "Integration"
    a) a solution to racial imbalance
    b) toolies and sociologists living in same neighborhood
    c) method for finding the area under a curve

    ANSWER: Answer c) is correct.

13. Define "Significant Figures"
    a) $1,000,000
    b) 36-21-36
    c) the leftmost non-zero digits to rightmost non-zero digits of a number.
    d) AMEX up $1\frac{1}{8}$; Dow Jones up $\frac{7}{8}$

    ANSWER: Sadly, only c) is the correct answer. For example, answer a) has only one "significant figure."

14. Define "D. C. Current"
    a) the Electric and Power Company in the Nation's Capital
    b) a constant supply of electricity, like from a battery
    c) an expression that causes you to grind your teeth
    d) a punk rock band

    ANSWER: Toolies will pick c) just because they don't like the other answers.

TOOLIES

15. Define "CAD"
    a) A person without gentlemanly instincts; a scoundrel
    b) A big car, unlike the ones toolies own
    c) Acronym for Computer Assisted Design

    ANSWER: Answer c) is the toolie choice

16. Define "A Light Day"
    a) A couple phone calls, check the mail, a little lunch, then take off the rest of the day to play golf
    b) The opposite of a dark and gloomy day
    c) Just guessing here, but—anything less than about a 500 pound day
    d) 16,000,000,000 miles

    ANSWER: Answer d), the distance travelled by light in twenty-four hours, is the predominant toolie response.

17. It's time for lunch. You stop in at a hoagie/submarine shop and order the house special turkey and roast beef combo, with the following instructions...
    a) Hold the onions.
    b) Hold the alfalfa sprouts
    c) Hold the house dressing (mayonnaise will be fine).
    d) On white bread.

    ANSWER: Score one point for each letter checked.

18. Which is heavier—a pound of feathers or a pound of rocks?
    a) a pound of feathers
    b) a pound of rocks
    c) neither
    d) where?

    ANSWER: a) is not only wrong, it's pitiful. Answer b) is not pitiful, just wrong. Answer c) is the time-honored correct answer to this question, so you deserve credit for selecting this answer. Answer d)

TOOLIES

shows that you realize that a load of feathers measuring, say, one pound on the moon will outweigh a pound of rocks back on earth by about five pounds. This is an obnoxious detail, but you do receive extra credit for thinking like a toolie if you answered d).

19. Upon being seated for dinner at a restaurant, you first...
    a) Leave napkin on table, order a cocktail, and engage in pleasant conversation.
    b) Place napkin in lap and order dinner.
    c) Unfold napkin, stick it in your collar, and wait for your BBQ ribs.
    d) Immediately unfold napkin, remove mechanical pencil from your shirt pocket, and start sketching drawings and calculations on your napkin.

ANSWER: d) is correct. CAUTION: This practice is frowned upon at restaurants that use linen napkins.

20. Referring to the staircase shown in the figure below: Neglecting air friction and assuming Poisson's ratio for Titanium to be .34, would it take more energy to walk around the staircase in direction A or direction B?
    a) Direction A
    b) Direction B
    c) .34
    d) No

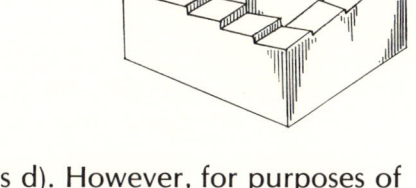

ANSWER: The correct answer is d). However, for purposes of scoring on this test, give yourself full credit for responding as a toolie if you answered either c) or d).

21. Coal Smut, Inc.'s manufacturing facility, shown above, was recently cited for failing to comply with the State Air Quality Control Board's "Particulate Emissions Standards." Your immediate reaction upon hearing this news is...
    a) Sue the bastards.
    b) Far out! Check out those chimneys.
    c) Have somebody from our environmental engineering design staff contact them immediately. There must be some work in this for us somewhere.

ANSWER: c) is the usual toolie choice.

TOOLIES

22. Is the glass shown in the figure at right half empty or half full? (Be careful. The wrong response here may keep you out of the Peace Corps).
    a) Half empty
    b) Half full
    c) No
    d) I get it. This is a trick question. Right? That isn't a glass; it's a plastic cup.

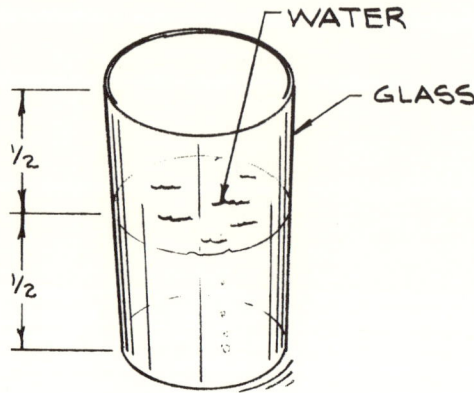

ANSWER: Part credit for choosing either answer a) or b). No credit for choosing answer d). (Toolies may be sticklers for details; but they're not complete jerks). Toolies will observe that the glass is neither half full nor half empty. It is completely full—the bottom half is full of water and the top half is full of air. Answer c) is the toolie choice.

INTERPRETATION OF TEST SCORES
Aptitude Test Score: Not Many Points

If you didn't score many points—and those who didn't know who I'm talking to—you simply do not have a toolie aptitude. You have little appreciation for the order of things in the universe. You rarely understand what goes on around you. You lack any really worthwhile goals. You will never make any significant contribution to the world you live in. You will become very successful and extremely wealthy.

Aptitude Test Score: Pretty Many Points

If you scored pretty many points *but at any time attempted to go back and add them up,* who are you trying to kid? No real toolie would ever go through such an effort. You have a good aptitude for being an accountant, a hair engineer, or a social scientist.

If you scored pretty many points—you haven't actually counted them, but you're sure you did—you have a toolie aptitude. You do have an appreciation for the order of things in the universe. Though you rarely like what you see, you have a good understanding for things that are going on around you. You often make contributions to the quality of life around you. You usually know what you're doing and there is a sense of direction to your life. You will never be wealthy. But, at least you'll know why.

Aptitude Test Score: A Whole Lot Of Points

Geeksville. You are a 24-hour-a-day toolie. Your motto is "Numbers are my life." You naively think that when people around you yawn it's because they didn't get enough sleep last night. You believe that anything worth doing is worth doing right...on a computer. To you, actions speak louder than words. But then, wall-mounted certificates speak louder than actions.

Contact your family physician immediately.

CHAPTER 6

The Real World Paradox

IF THE RESULTS of your Toolie Aptitude Test proved positive, you may be one of a select group of individuals who accurately claims to be domiciled in The Real World.

It is ironic that toolies' identification with the real world persists in spite of (or perhaps because of) their lengthy studies of patently ideal circumstances. The toolie education relies heavily on analyses of things like "ideal gases," "frictionless bearings," and "absolute vacuums"—none of which actually exist in the real world. In fact, it is probably not stretching things much to suggest that toolies couldn't even exist if they couldn't regularly make such bogus assumptions about the world around them. But, somehow, toolies have so far avoided being lumped in with that seemingly endless list of people who are told that they aren't living in the real world.

Since the late sixties, one group after another has been notified of its exclusion from the real world. For a time it was inaccurately presumed that those rendering such notification were themselves real world inhabitants. The facts, however, simply did not support such a presumption.

Today there is much information available regarding which segments of the population are *not* living in the real world (see Real World Residency List). For example, we know from analysis of readily available empirical data that real world occupants are *not* executive directors of large corporations, are *not* rich, do *not* hold multiple doctoral degress from Ivy League universities, will never win the New Jersey State Lottery, do *not* marry Miss America, and do *not* spend their winters in the Virgin Islands. But, contrary to earlier schools of thought, it is now known that real worlders also are not *necessarily* starving, uneducated, indigent slobs. This revelation was an important breakthrough towards providing a much needed morale boost to the toolie community.

Although there is substantial information available describing the characteristics of those who don't live in the real world, there is scarcely little telling us exactly who does live there. Every once in a while distinct traits, such as "having one's feet on the ground," have been isolated in laboratory conditions as being "attributable to those living in the real world." However, such traits have thus far been mostly speculative in nature, and indeed, further research is essential. (Indeed, further research is always essential).

Not only are the personal characteristics of real worlders still quite vague, but in fact even the geographic proximity of the real world has never been adequately described. One hypothesis suggests that in order to locate it, one merely needs to identify those who "have their feet on the ground," and simply look under their feet. However, since these tests (as described above) to isolate such real world traits have generally been conducted in laboratory settings, it is the laboratories that keep showing up in these tests as the real world. It is little wonder that only lab technicians and diseased rats strongly support this hypothesis.

Some preliminary steps have been taken in recent years to pinpoint the location of the real world. As this book goes to press, tests are not complete, but we have learned the following: The first definitive results showed that the real world is, without question, not in Hollywood. Follow-up studies have proven that it is not in

California at all. This, of course, does not come as a surprise to most people.

It has been known for some time now that the real world also does not encompass Washington, D.C. Latest theories suggest that it is somewhere between Washington, D.C. and California, perhaps near Dayton. But so far results are still quite sketchy.

What is certain, however, is that most toolies are, if not full time residents, at least in intermittent contact with the real world. This fact is supported by reams and reams of quantified statistical data far too lengthy, boring, inaccurate, and, well, meaningless to be itemized here. But you know it and that's what counts.

REAL WORLD RESIDENCY LIST

Definitely Not Living In The Real World

According To:

Definitely Not Living In The Real World	According To:
College professors	Students
Students	Townies, graduates
Professional Athletes	Unanimous
Rich People	Poor People
Whites	Non-whites
Non-Whites	Whites
Politicians	Journalists, Voters
Journalists, Reporters	Politicians, Voters
ET	Earthlings
Management	Labor
Anyone who is employed	Anyone unemployed
Foreigners	Americans
Americans	Foreigners
Rock singers	Mothers, other Rock Singers
Hair dressers	People with heads
Movie stars	Unanimous

TOOLIES

The Real World should not be confused with the Ideal World. I'm not sure exactly why not—but it probably shouldn't. An artsy-crafty's definition of an Ideal World is a "world in which all men and women—regardless of their race, creed or slogan—live side-by-side (albeit each in his or her own space) in an ecologically balanced, and fiscally responsible, environment." Toolies, on the other hand, would describe an Ideal World as one at standard temperature and pressure (STP) where air friction is negligible and voltage sources are constant. The list below gives a sampling of the many idealizations that toolies use before they start to tackle any toolie problem.

IDEAL WORLD DESIGN AIDS
...Or "48 assumptions guaranteed to simplify toolie calculations"

(see diagram on the next page)

1. Negligible AIR FRICTION
2. Infinitely Long BEAM
3. Perfectly Rigid BEAM
4. Weightless BEAM
5. Frictionless BEARING
6. Perfect BLACK BODY
7. Perfectly Flexible CABLE
8. Weightless CABLE
9. Perfect CIRCLE
10. Non-COMPRESSIBLE (anything)
11. Perfect CONDUCTOR
12. CONTINUUM
13. Continuous DISTRIBUTION
14. Perfectly Random DISTRIBUTION
15. 100% EFFICIENCY
16. Perfect ELASTICITY
17. Irrotational (FLUID) Flow
18. Perfect FLUID
19. Negligible FRICTION
20. Ideal GAS
21. Perfect GAS
22. Zero HEAD LOSS
23. (Perfectly) Reversible HEAT FLOW
24. Perfect HEAT SINK
25. Perfect INELASTICITY
26. Perfect INSULATOR
27. Frictionless Sliding JOINT
28. Frictionless Ball JOINT
29. Frictionless Hinged JOINT
30. Infinitely Long LINE
31. Perfectly Straight LINE
32. All MASS concentrated in center
33. Perfectly Plastic MATERIAL
34. Infinite MASS
35. Negligible MASS
36. Simultaneous OCCURENCES
37. Isothermal PROCESS
38. Perfect REFLECTOR
39. Instantaneous SPEED
40. Steady STATE (anything)
41. Ideal Clamped SUPPORT
42. Continuous SURFACE
43. Frictionless SURFACE
44. Negligible TRANSIENTS
45. 100% TRANSPARENT
46. Weightless TRUSS
47. Absolute VACUUM
48. Constant VOLTAGE SOURCE

TOOLIES

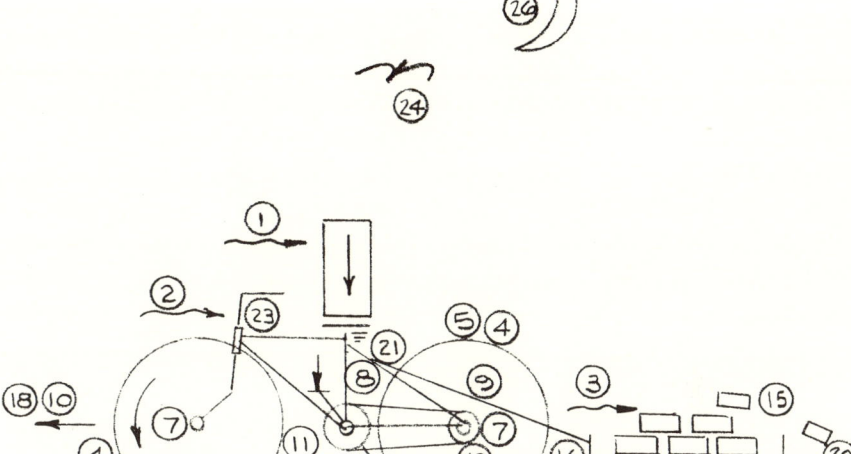

Free Body Diagram of Sample Problem

EXAMPLE OF PROBLEM SOLVING USING "IDEAL WORLD DESIGN AIDS" LIST

Sample Problem:

Determine how much work is done by pedaling a bicycle five times around a city block while towing a wagon loaded with one hundred pounds of bricks.

Assumptions:

1) Neglect wind friction against rider
2) Neglect wind friction against bike
3) Neglect wind friction against wagon
4) Assume bike tires filled with non-compressible ideal gas
5) Assume bike tires constructed of perfectly elastic rubber
6) Neglect rolling friction between bike tires and pavement
7) Assume both bike wheels pivot about frictionless bearings
8) Assume wagon handle is attached to bike with ideal frictionless pinned joint

TOOLIES

9) Assume wagon handle stem is a perfectly rigid beam of negligible weight and of zero cross-sectional area

10) Assume bike travels at constant velocity, neglecting any frictions due to application of brakes

11) Neglect friction between bike chain and drive sprocket

12) Neglect friction between bike chain and rear sprocket

13) Neglect friction between individual chain links

14) Neglect rolling friction between wagon wheels and pavement

15) Assume all bricks in wagon remain static (do not shift position) during the trip

16) Assume an ideal frictionless ball joint between wagon handle stem and wagon body

17) Assume start and finish lines are at the same elevation (relative to the center of the earth—where all of the earth's mass may be assumed to be concentrated)

18) Assume bike velocity is negligible relative to the speed of light

19) Assume all wagon wheels pivot on ideal frictionless axles

20) Assume weight loss (from perspiration, falling bricks, worn tires, etc.) is negligible

21) Assume a frictionless, perfectly rigid rider support system (i.e. the seat doesn't squeak)

22) Assume wagon rolls on perfectly circular, infinitely rigid, non-compressible frictionless wheels

23) Assume handle bar stem is attached to bike frame with a perfect frictionless hinged joint

24) Assume weight gain (from accumulated dust particles, bird droppings, hitch hikers, etc.) is negligible

25) Neglect friction due to wheels sliding around corners

26) Assume lunar gravitational forces on bike remain constant during trip

Calculation:

FORMULA: Work = Force x Distance Traveled
ANSWER: Work = 0

Therefore, NO work is done.

COEFFICIENTS

Back in the old days there were very few printing presses and there were even fewer toolies who knew how to write. One of the first toolies who tried to write was Sir Isaac Newton. As you can see from the title page of his famous book, Sir Isaac Newton was not a very good speller—but at least he did get published.

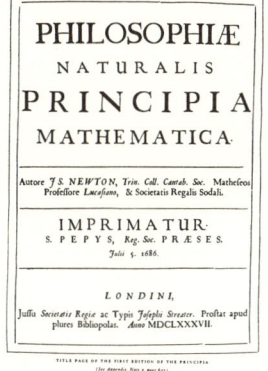

Since his was the only toolie book printed for a couple hundred years, nearly all fundamental science and engineering principles studied by toolies were based on what came to be known as Newton's laws.

Unfortunately, Newton's laws were all based on an assumption (which was widely held in those days by kings, knights, and people whose first name was "sir") that the world was ideal. This led to his writing such ridiculous laws as: for every action there is an opposite and equal reaction. Much to their dismay, people like General Custer discovered that this law was not exactly true in the real world.

To avoid going back and changing all the old laws of science, modern toolies have learned to use "coefficients." (Artsy-craftsies call them "fudge factors," but "coefficients" definitely has a much better ring to it.) So today we might say that for every action there is an opposite and equal reaction times coefficient C. Granted, you may have to stare at the serious end of the arrows from four thousand hostile Indians to determine the precise value of coefficient C, but at least your equations will be technically correct. Albert Einstein proposed using a value of 186,000 miles per second for C, "just to be sure." Since nobody understood what he was talking about, he was declared a "genius" and awarded the Nobel Prize.

CHAPTER 7

Toolie Fields

MECHANICAL ENGINEERING

UNLESS TOLD OTHERWISE (and often not even then), the entire world assumes that if you are an engineer, you *must* be a mechanical engineer. Everyone takes for granted that all engineers can fix their neighbor's cuckoo clocks, their cars, their broken lawn mowers, or blenders, or their children's toys, and that with only a moment's notice design a framastatic widget thingamabob to solve whatever other problems they may have. To be sure, these neighbors feel quite betrayed if you dare tell them, "Sorry, "I'm a *chemical* engineer. I know nothing about bicycles."

Throughout the ages the most recognized toolies have been the "ME's." Leonardo, Newton, Archimedes. The Wright brothers, Carnot, Edison. Errickson, Franklin, Fulton, and Whitney. All ME's (at least in spirit).

So it is not alarming that ME's are jolted when they first find out that they will spend their entire professional careers designing heating, ventilating, and air conditioning (HVAC) ductwork systems

TOOLIES

for an endless parade (i.e. continuum) of building plans. Can you imagine Leonardo laying out HVAC ductwork? No way.

By the end of his career, the average mechanical engineer will have designed between 16 and 16.24 thousand miles of ductwork and approximately 73.5 thousand miles of pipelines. Since all pipes are round and all ducts are rectangular, it isn't any wonder that by the afternoon of the first day on the job, all mechanical engineering work begins to look the same. And nothing ever occurs to change this perception.

CIVIL ENGINEERING

Civil Engineering is the backbone of all the engineering fields. Approximately 62.8 percent of all civil engineering graduates switched to civil after starting in another major.

Civil engineering was the first of the recognized engineering disciplines to depart from the design of military and war machinery (such as cross bows, catapults, and fortresses) to non-military, or "civil" work. From all evidence available, it was fortunate for everyone concerned that civil engineers did not (or were not allowed to) work around things that can hurt people.

Civil engineering is most notable as the only engineering field that exclusively designs things that *do not move*. From all evidence available, it is also fortunate for all of us that civil engineers do not design things that can move.

This is also the only toolie discipline in which those entering the field have absolutely no delusions about how interesting the field is. Civil engineering candidates don't expect their jobs to be very interesting—and they're right.

In a recent toolie poll, one hundred civil engineers were asked to describe their "most interesting day on the job." Ninety-three responses were left blank. The remaining seven indicated that being included in the survey was the most exciting thing that they could remember *ever* happening to them.

DRAFTING

Draftspersons are an essential spoke in the toolie wheel. A popular draftsmen's saying suggests, "Engineers are only draftspersons who can't draw."

TOOLIES

Most draftsmen start off happy enough to be the real line workers of the toolie fields. Invariably after a short time (usually about four days on the job), draftsmen one by one convince themselves (perhaps accurately) that the most important product of all toolie work is the finished drawing. After all, "isn't that what the client is paying for?" And it therefore follows that they know more, think more, do more, are less replaceable, work harder, and are generally more valuable than anyone else who has ever walked through an engineering office.

These, of course, are the same infallible people whose work necessitated the invention and proliferation of the ubiquitous electric eraser.

ARCHITECTURE

If engineers are draftsmen who can't draw, then architects are engineers who can't do math.

Architects make up the rogue element among the toolies. This is the only group of toolies that can regularly be found wearing beards or eating granola bars.

Architecture is the glory job among toolie professions. Although knowing *nothing* about a building's design or construction other than its color, the architect invariably receives first credit and top billing as the buiding's designer.

Architects are, in a sense, the "general contractors" of the toolie business. It is they who coordinate the efforts of the many other toolie trades on construction design projects and who have full responsibility for that most important of all architectural tasks—ensuring that the plans of the various fields are all on the same size drawing paper and can easily be stapled together.

61

TOOLIES

NUCLEAR ENGINEERING

Without a doubt, the most impressive-*sounding* toolie field is nuclear engineering. Even though there is absolutely no reasonable correlation whatsoever between the two, if you ever, EVER, tell someone that you are a nuclear engineer, you sure as hell better be able to stop his toilet from running over!

In recent years the nuclear engineering field has taken a beating from outsiders who keep letting little things (like the danger of radioactive isotopes filling the air and turning their offspring into one-armed, four-eyed mutants) influence their attitudes towards nuclear engineers.

Because none of them signed up for such harassment, a lot of "nukies" end up leaving engineering altogether and become lawyers. As lawyers they still get harassed a lot, but at least then they deserve it.

SANITARY ENGINEERS

It is true that sanitary engineers are only toolies by name, and otherwise fill none of the criteria for being toolies. However, sanitary engineers (a.k.a. garbage men, refuse collectors) are included here because quite frankly, they raise the average.

They are paid better than nearly all real engineers, and although it is true that they may be looked down upon by some, it is also abundantly evident that respect can be bought. Sanitary engineers work excellent hours (approximately three hours a day); drive company owned vehicles (garbage trucks); operate state-of-the-art equipment (hydraulic trash compactors); have first refusal rights on all consumer seconds; retire young with excellent pensions (as well as part interest in "antique goods" companies); and get to spend a large amount of their time out of the office doing "field" work.

INDUSTRIAL ENGINEERS

What happens if a person is inclined towards business, accounting, bookkeeping, or management, but due to various genetic circumstances beyond his control, is born a toolie? Simple. He becomes an industrial engineer.

TOOLIES

Industrial engineering is the only toolie field that actually takes transfers *from* civil engineering.

Although industrial engineering is often a gratifying profession, it frequently requries a lot of soul-searching. Industrial engineers are often burdened with the task of determining, for example, whether it is better to buy one widget-making machine that lasts ten years and eliminates ten artsy-craftsies, or to buy another machine that costs less and lasts longer but eliminates only eight artsy-craftsies. Most industrial engineers, after spending ample time "researching" the options, eventually decide to do both.

SURVEYING

Surveying is easily the oldest and most laid-back toolie field. In only slightly simplified terms, surveying is the practice of finding an area of ground and then measuring it.

The ground, as a rule, doesn't move very fast and, as a rule, neither do surveyors.

Far and away, the toolies with the best tans are the surveyors. Unlike all other toolies, surveyors do not work on rainy days. Or on snowy days. Or on exceptionally cold or hot days. Or on days containing the letter "s." The prevailing attitude among surveyors is that the ground will probably be in more or less the same place whenever they eventually get around to doing their measuring, so what's the hurry?

Surveyors are also the most visible toolies, often being found standing in the center of busy highways wearing luminescent orange vests. This is a practice that would be utterly condemnable in any other toolie field.

The pride of any surveyor is his transit. And rightly so. No tool is more closely associated with any toolie profession or more aptly suggests the very derivation of the word "toolie" than the surveyors' transit.

CHEMICAL ENGINEERING

The chemical engineering curriculum is generally regarded among toolies as the most academically demanding of all toolie curricula.

TOOLIES

Of any ten people entering college with intentions of becoming chemical engineers, six of these will switch to mechanical engineering (and four of *them* will subsequently transfer into civil engineering), one will drop out of school completely and eventually become a wealthy corporate executive, two will go on to medical school and become doctors, and one will actually become a practicing chemical engineer.

Partially because of their high attrition rate, but mostly because they often have to be coerced into working side-by-side with chemists and doctors, chemical engineers are traditionally the highest salaried of the true toolies.

ELECTRICAL ENGINEERING

Prospective electrical engineers usually think that some day they will be doing something like designing complex circuits which will manipulate robotic arms on extraterrestrial space vehicles for the good of mankind.

Ha! More often than not they end up spending most of their time figuring out how many duplex outlets should be in a living room wall, or whether to use direct or indirect lighting in the den, or some other calculation of similarly important socio-economic impact.

"Double E's," as they usually refer to themselves, are the quietest and most "insulated" of all toolies, and toolies, quite frankly, are not generally regarded as overly boisterous or outgoing in the first place.

Electrical engineers are a bit of an enigma to most people, primarily because they have invented their own vocabulary rather than use the one the rest of us rely on. All toolies, for example, measure things, but while civil engineers might measure things in "pounds per foot" and mechanical engineers might measure things in "pounds per minute," EE's will measure things in "Henrys," "Farrads," and "Watts," which comes out sounding more like some fly-by-night law firm than units of measure.

COMPUTER SCIENCE

The newest and fastest growing toolie field is computer science. During its infancy (about four years ago), almost anyone remotely associated with computers was a toolie. But these days you can't always tell.

A lot of real computer scientists are justifiably concerned that the field is becoming infiltrated with Word Processor Input Technicians (typists) and the like who—let's face it—just don't meet toolie standards. Presumably these less desirables—who can be identified by their lively wardrobes, their active recreational lifestyles, and their leaving the office at 5:00 sharp—will be weeded out in time.

A true computer scientist's work is never done. According to any computer scientist there has apparently never been a computer program that couldn't be improved. So, they interminably want to make them shorter, faster, easier, more powerful, friendlier, interactive, retroactive, hyperbolic, extravehicular. Asking a computer programmer to finish—no, I mean really FINISH—a program for you is probably the most frustrating thing you will ever do.

A lot of computer scientists have bladder problems. This is because they don't dare take a break during the day for fear that they may miss the development of the next two generations of computer equipment they are working with.

But the best thing about being a computer scientist is that they don't need to know much math. The only numbers they use are zero and one. This apparently has something to do with some kind of memory problem—but we really shouldn't make fun of them.

PROFESSIONAL REGISTRATION

At some point in your career, you may want to become licensed in your state as a toolie. In addition to its other less obvious benefits, registration allows you to hang yet another certificate on your office wall. If you are really into being a toolie (as you probably are), you will want to become registered in several different states, many of which just a short while ago you didn't even know existed.

TOOLIES

Since nearly all states have reciprocity agreements, multiple state registrations require little more than the payment of the necessary fees. This allows the really gung-ho toolie to nearly cover his wall with registration certificates from the various states.

Lest you chance appearing ostentatious (a particularly untoolie-like characteristic), or making it appear that K-Mart was having a sale on toolie licenses, it is suggested that you limit your interstate registrations to those states which you can actually locate on a United States map.

There are, of course, other reasons for becoming licensed. Most are merely smoke screens for the true reason—making more money. The subject of money is considered inappropriate for general discussion in toolie circles, and should never be brought up in mixed company (i.e. with artsy-craftsies).

Toolies, to a man/woman, are philosophically opposed to labor unions. Whenever it comes up, toolies will either avoid confrontation (unquestionably the preferred action), or will side with management. Being from the real world, toolies fully appreciate and understand the circumstances that lead to the formation of labor unions. But once formed, unions ideally should be immediately disbanded.

Instead of unions, toolies prefer "professional registration" or "licensing."

In general, to become licensed to practice as a toolie one must be a graduate from a tool school, have several years experience working for another registered toolie, own at least one mechanical pencil, and pass a statewide toolie examination. (Some localities will also require that you be able to demonstrate a familiarity with the operation of a clipboard. I suggest you consult your local authorities for licensing requirements in your area.) In most states registration as a Professional Engineer (PE) actually requires a second statewide examination after serving a necessary penance period as an "Engineer-in-Training" (EIT).

EIT'S

Those uninitiated to the toolie world may find it difficult to understand why, *after* four years of rigorous studies and endless problem sets and examinations at one of the top colleges in the country; *after* receiving a BS degree from a supposedly "accredited" university; *after* several years of professional experience working for a certified licensed toolie; *after* passing an eight-hour long comprehensive nationwide examination covering nearly every subject ever encountered by a practicing toolie; and *after* abstaining from the near occasion of culture for at least four years, it is then necessary to ordain such a person as an Engineer-*in-training*.

But, those same people probably wouldn't even understand why it is necessary to fail one out of every three of the engineering school graduates who take that examination. It's really quite simple (the explanation, not the examination).

Engineers-in-Training fill an important position in the toolie hierarchy. The first level in the hierarchy is made up of EIT's. The second level is made up of professional engineers (PE's). As it turns out, these are the only two levels in the hierarchy, and to eliminate either would seriously upset the equilibrium of the hierarchy (i.e. the sum of the forces in the Y direction would not equal zero). And toolies never like to upset things. Much less themselves.

The engineering profession is unique in the use of an appellation such as engineer-in-training to denote such a high level of professional accomplishment. This self-demeaning title is indicative of toolies' ongoing endeavor to keep everything and everyone (including themselves) in their proper places. Perhaps "Associate Engineer," "Grade I Engineer," "Engineer-Class A," or just "Engineer" would be okay. But "Engineer-in-Training?!" Kind of sounds like "Bag Boy in Training."

In contrast, upon graduation from medical school, one is properly called a doctor. Sure, there are internships, residencies, and further examinations, but they are all called doctors. No one would want someone called a "Doctor-in-Training" to monitor his vital signs.

Upon passing the bar exam, one is called a lawyer. Who in his right mind would want to have an "Attorney-in-Training" handling his important matters? (For that matter, who in his right mind would want *any* attorney to handle his important matters?)

TOOLIES

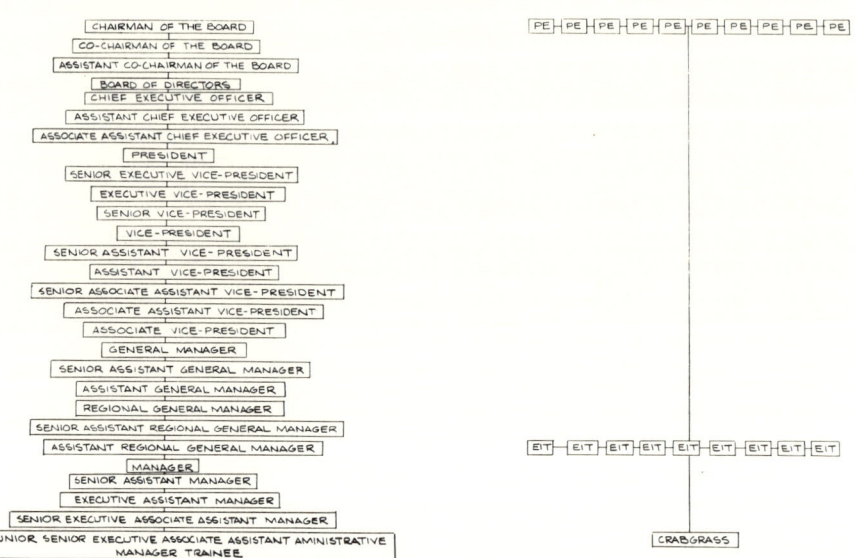

NON-TOOLIE ORGANIZATIONAL HIERARCHY   TOOLIE ORGANIZATIONAL HIERARCHY

LICENSING EXAMINATION

The final step in the registration process is to become a licensed professional. This is achieved by passing yet another examination. Since this will be the last examination you will ever take, the board of examiners goes to great lengths to make sure that the examination is fair and accurately anticipates questions which will come up daily in your career as a licensed professional toolie.

Typical of such everyday problems, for example, is the following question which was undoubtedly taken from a recent licensing exam:

> "What is the volume of the solid generated when a three inch diameter chocolate doughnut is swung on a 6.5 meter long string around a stationary flag pole? Assume air friction is negligible, the icing temperature is 22 deg Celsius at barometric pressure 29 inches mercury and the modulus of elasticity of the string is 100 kpsi. Round off answers to 4 significant figures."

There is hardly a professional toolie alive who hasn't run into this or a similiar problem sometime during his career. Most likely when he took his licensing exam.

CATCH 7 PI

While asking extremely practical questions such as the one above, it is also important that the examination be fairly difficult, even for the experienced toolie. This is necessary because only by weeding out another third of these professional toolie candidates can the ultimate purpose of the licensing procedure, "selective perpetuation," be served.

In its simplest terms, selective perpetuation is the practice of making it so difficult to become registered that only those who are licensed professionals are qualified to determine that, for most toolie work, a licensed professional is actually *not* necessary. Knowledgeable toolies refer to this particular arrangement as "Catch 7 Pi."

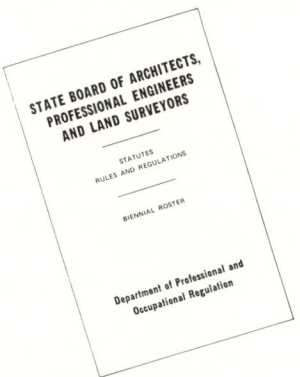

PURPOSE OF LICENSING

The popular explanation for the necessity of professional licensing is that, without such a requirement, public safety would be jeopardized because buildings and structures would then be designed and built by artsy-craftsies.

Houses would be designed by historians. Sociologists would be designing our hydroelectric power plants. And grocery clerks would be designing our suspension bridges during their free time. All this, obviously, would lead to a particularly unsafe environment.

But some people still confuse registration as an attempt to weed out low quality from high quality work, rather than to distinguish between toolies and artsy-craftsies. Quality, to be direct, has nothing to do with it.

TOOLIES

This is best illustrated by appreciating the fact that, in most states, registration as a professional toolie makes no distinction between the various toolie fields. This means that a registered first-year civil engineer, for example, who has spent his entire two months of professional work designing sludge removal piping, is professionally licensed to design a nuclear power station, a field which we will pretend (wink, wink) he knows nothing about.

The proper explanation, of course, is that this registered professional toolie would be 1) smart enough to recognize that he doesn't know how to design a nuclear reactor, and 2) ethically bound by the Toolie Code not to design a nuclear plant if he were asked to.

The corollary to this explanation is, however, that an unlicensed artsy-craftsy (for example, our grocery clerk) would be 1) too ignorant to realize that he doesn't know how to design a nuclear reactor (what?) and 2) too dishonest or unethical to admit as much if he were paid to design one. This corollary is not real popular with grocery clerks.

Both sides of this argument point out the true purpose of professional registration. Each is based on the usually valid assumption that there is a buyer somewhere (most likely an artsy-craftsy working on his imbeeay) who is equally prepared to pay either a first-year civil engineer or a grocery clerk, whichever is the low bidder, to design a nuclear power station.

THE PUBLIC SAFETY

It would be negligent not to acknowledge here that toolie licensing is not required for all toolie endeavors. Through the years, laws regarding professional registration have gradually been modified and interpreted by the courts so that, today, toolie licensing is now only mandatory when the safety of the public is at stake.

This explanation for toolie licensing is quite commendable. And buried deep in it is the reason why you have to have a license to design the piping to your neighbor's new hot tub, while no licensing is necessary to design automobiles in which thousands of people die every month.

Of course, it is impossible to come up with any conceivable explanation for how the public could possibly benefit from the licensing of architects. At best, the licensing of architects could only protect the public from ugly buildings. But one quick look around will quickly dispel any notion that that goal is being accomplished.

LANDING WORK, or getting jobs when neither price nor quality is considered

Now that you are a certified, licensed, registered toolie, your occupational emphasis will have to change. You are now in a position to help your firm land work. Landing work is one of the most important elements in the equation of business success. To be successful at landing jobs, it is important that you understand the protocol and procedures of professional toolieism and how to take advantage of your (until now unknown) assets, an area in which the standard toolie training has failed to educate you.

```
TOOLIE PRICE LIST

$10/HR    DESIGN IT.

$20/HR    DESIGN IT AND PREPARE PLANS
          SPECIFIC ENOUGH FOR ME TO UNDERSTAND.

$40/HR    DESIGN IT AND PREPARE PLANS
          SPECIFIC ENOUGH FOR ME TO DESCRIBE
          IT TO YOU.

$80/HR    DESIGN IT AND PREPARE PLANS
          SPECIFIC ENOUGH FOR YOU TO DESCRIBE
          IT TO SOMEONE ELSE.

$160/HR   DESIGN IT AND PREPARE PLANS
          SPECIFIC ENOUGH FOR IT TO BE BUILT
          BY SOMEONE THAT NEITHER YOU
          NOR I HAVE MET.

$320/HR   DESIGN IT AND PREPARE PLANS
          SPECIFIC ENOUGH FOR IT TO BE BUILT
          BY SOMEONE THAT NEITHER YOU
          NOR I NOR MY LAWYER NEED
          EVER WORRY ABOUT MEETING.
```

TOOLIES

I'M OK; YOU'RE OK

By virtue of your extensive educational and professional training, and as is evidenced by your degree, your job title, and your professional registration, you unquestionably are fully qualified to perform your toolie job, whatever it may be: designing a building, engineering a heating system, or programming a computer. Damn, you're good. However, the exact same thing can be said about the millions of other toolies who are going after the same work as you.

This differs, for example, from the auto repair business where, given the same list of symptoms of a car's problem, no two artsy-craftsies will replace the same part, attempt to solve the same problem, take the same amount of time, or charge the same amount. If there is one thread of continuity between such artsy-craftsy operations, it is that your problem will not be fully remedied when the job is complete and you will have been overcharged for the effort. But at least with artsy-craftsies, you know at the outset that you will be overcharged, and by referring to a printed price list you can even tell in advance just how badly you're going to be taken. With toolies, however, you will never know how much a job will cost until after you have selected the toolie to do the work—and by then it's too late.

Toolies do not issue "price lists" or bid for work. Bidding, as you know, is tacky. It is considered unprofessional (as well as self-destructive) for one professional to try to undersell another professional. So toolie services generally are not selected based on prices, and, in many cases, it is actually against the law to consider price in the selection of toolie services.

Also, unlike other professions where no two opinions are ever the same, when a thousand qualified toolies are asked the same technical question, say, to determine the diameter of a concrete column that is necessary to support a roof, they will all give only one answer. And it will be correct. This is necessarily true.

Because the product, and the quality of the product, are the same from each toolie, toolie work is rarely selected based on quality of workmanship.

So, since all toolies generally turn out the same quality of finished work, and since the price of work is considered inappropriate

TOOLIES

as a selection criterion, the awarding of design contracts is a most interesting procedure. Factor into this that most design contracts are awarded by artsy-craftsy buyers (who don't even pretend to know anything about toolie work) and the procedure almost becomes incomprehensible.

RESUME AMPLIFICATION

It is only once you, as a professional toolie, realize that neither competence nor price is considered in the awarding of toolie contracts, that you may then concentrate your work-hunting efforts where they will do the most good.

The primary criterion upon which one toolie (or toolie firm) is chosen over another is recent past experience on a similar job. The second (and only other) basis is a showing of how much of that experience was gained while working for this particular buyer. This, as you might expect, makes things tough for the young toolie (or toolie firm) that is trying to get started in the business. (That, of course, is the whole idea.) This minor obstacle is easily overcome by practicing the fundamental principles of "resume amplification."

Resume amplification is the process by which any and every event in your lifetime may be construed as a scientific and/or educational experience, the most relevant of which not only occurred within the last month, but was performed for whomever is awarding the contract under consideration.

EXAMPLE OF RESUME AMPLIFICATION

Job Description
Preparation of plans and specifications for installation of new elevator shaft in existing U.S. Post Office building in Washington, D.C.

Sample Resume

a) Name & Title:
   MICHAEL MONTGOMERY, Civil Engineer
b) Project Assignment:
   PROJECT ENGINEER
c) Name of Firm with which associated:
   MM DESIGN COLLABORATIVE
d) Education:
   BSCE, Ohio State University
   Post Grad Lib Studies: Massachusetts Institute of Technology
e) Active Registration:
   PE Candidate/Civil Engineering
f) Other Experience and Qualifications Relevant to the Proposed Project:

Mr. Montgomery provides MM Design Collaborative with nearly ten years of progressive experience in the design and analysis of structural shaft systems. Mr. Montgomery has an extensive working knowledge of elevator operations, including several years "hands-on" experience in the field.

In addition to his engineering background, Mr. Montgomery is also an accomplished elevator draftsman and has authored and published numerous technical reports on elevator structures.

In a recently completed Post Office project initiated by Mr. Montgomery, the entire design package was delivered on time and under budget.

Most recently, Mr. Montgomery has acted as chief engineer in charge of design review of construction for an eight million dollar U.S. Post Office building facility, including the installation of four 2000 lb. gross weight elevator systems.

INTERPRETATION OF THE PRECEDING SAMPLE RESUME

a) Name & Title:
   Mike Montgomery, Draftsman

b) Project Assignment:
   He will do most of the drafting but we will bill for his time as though he were the project engineer.

c) Name of Firm:
   Michael Montgomery Design Collaborative

d) Education:
   Since getting my degree in civil engineering, I read a couple of library books which, I understand, are on file at MIT's library in Cambridge, Massachusetts.

e) Active Registration:
   After I get around to taking the EIT exam, if I happen to pass it, I then hope to some day take the PE exam.

f) Other experience and Qualifications Relevant to the Proposed Project:
   First of all, Mike Montgomery **is** MM Design Collaborative. If Mike can somehow land this contract he will surely have to collaborate with anyone he can find to get the job done.

   Ten years ago (well, actually only seven years), Mike knew nothing at all about the design of elevators. Today he knows that elevators have "shafts." This is called "progressive experience."

   He has been riding elevators since he was a kid. For years now he has even pushed the buttons himself. This is known as "hands on" experience.

   Not only has he written graffiti on many elevator walls, but he also does his own illustrations "on elevator structures."

   Since he hasn't landed a job for months, he has spent considerable time recently staring out of his window watching the Post Office building across the street being built. This is known as "design and construction review."

   The last package Mike mailed through the U.S. Postal system arrived before Christmas and didn't cost as much as he thought it was going to cost.

   Note: Mike has never actually designed anything, much less an elevator.

CHAPTER 8

Excitement— Living Without It

CONTRARY TO POPULAR belief, a toolie does have a social life. Problem is, nobody knows who that toolie is.

Toolies tend to be, if nothing else, an extremely practical lot. Although practicality can, in many cases, turn out to be a lifesaving virtue, and is nearly always the most rationally defensible course which one can take, it is, nonetheless, a serious burden when trying to socialize.

Its consequences to the social development of the toolie are staggering. For example, when your arts and crafts college buddies get together in the dead of winter (as they surely will) and suggest that each of you first drink a keg of warm beer, then run through the neighborhood screaming vulgarities stark naked, after which you take refuge from security officers by spending the night in a large garbage dumpster while each of you relieves yourself therein, you will probably decline that extremely tempting invitation, reasoning that it wouldn't be altogether a practical thing to do. Such narrow-

TOOLIES

minded reasoning on your part will cause you to miss out on all sorts of fun as well as many opportunities to meet people. The effects of all these missed opportunities will surely take their toll.

This is not to suggest that toolies are not dynamic and fun people. It just takes a little longer for them to get warmed up. Toolies are, and always will be, great observers. Careful observation is one of the essential elements of the scientific method which so influences the toolie lifestyle. At a party the toolie will quietly stand (usually alone) while the rest of the partiers become more and more lively as the evening goes on. What the toolie is doing is observing. If, after careful scrutiny, it appears that it would be practical to join in on the revelry (i.e. when lives and property and prestige are not being jeopardized), the toolie will join in. Often, he will then become the life of the party as his long pent-up qualities are liberated (if only for a short time).

If, on the other hand, it would appear that to join in would not be practical (i.e. when dousing the hostess' cat with lighter fluid and setting it afire), the toolie will just continue to observe. It is, then, a good idea for the host or hostess to always invite at least one toolie to each party because the toolie will serve as an accurate barometer of the success of the party. But it is also clear, for obvious reasons, that toolies should not make up a very high percentage of the guest list (i.e. more than 3 percent would probably be pushing it).

TECHNICAL SOCIETY MEETINGS

The particular case where all the guests are, in fact, toolies, is a non-event known as a "Technical Society Meeting" at which only toolies (no guests, please) are in attendance. In short, a Technical Society Meeting is a slow-motion social anomaly in which a large number of grown professionals stand around in groups of no more than three (two being the preferred group size) observing each other observing each other.

After about an hour of this excitement—or roughly the amount of time necessary for the ice in the one mixed drink that you have nursed throughout this preliminary round of the meeting to completely disappear—all of the toolies then sit down to observe a single guest speaker.

The guest speaker will choose a topic to speak on about which no one else in the room knows anything. It seems to make little difference to most guest speakers that no one knows anything about the topic simply because no one *cares* about it.

When the guest speaker has finished speaking on the evening's topic he will signal those toolies who are still awake that it is time to go. Since you never know when you might be one of the few people left awake during such a meeting, it is important that you learn to recognize the signal. The universally accepted signal is that the guest speaker will abruptly change to a totally unrelated topic, saying something that sounds vaguely like a joke you think you heard in high school. He then will curl up one corner of one side of his mouth in a gesture not altogether distinguishable from some kind of a smile.

This signal marking the end to the night's event has worked for years for toolies and may soon be experimented with in other areas such as at concerts, plays, and sporting events.

SPORTING TOOLIES

"An intelligent player is not worth a damn if he's slow making moves."
        Major League Baseball Personnel Director

Perhaps.

TOOLIES

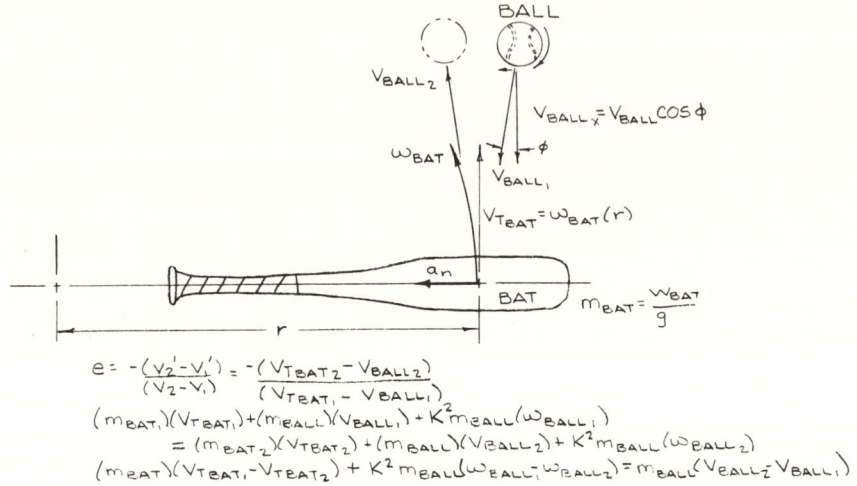

Although a reasonable corollary to the above quotation might be that an unintelligent player is worth even less than a damn if he's slow making moves, experience and bank accounts have taught us that is not always the case.

Contrary to popular belief, toolies do make excellent athletes... up to a point. Given similar levels of coordination and equal physiques, when a toolie and an artsy-craftsy are introduced to a sporting event at the same time, the initial advantage will nearly always go to the toolie. The toolie will quickly assimilate the rules of the event and will immediately grasp the nuances, strategies, and many of the "tricks" of the game.

The toolie, for example, will be the first to appreciate that with a certain rotation a baseball will curve over the plate; that by keeping his center of gravity low he will be the most difficult to tackle while carrying a football; or that conservation of linear and angular momentum will allow him to successfully complete his dive into the pool.

TOOLIES

In spite of this edge, toolies rarely turn into great athletes. A former college basketball coach and television commentator is quoted as saying, "Super-intelligent people can't be superb athletes. They're too aware." (To be sure, it would be presumptuous to generally classify all toolies as "super-intelligent." On the other hand, it is strongly suspected that the esteemed coach's idea of "super-intelligence" is probably light-years below what toolies would consider it to be.)

His point though is well taken. Although the recently indoctrinated toolie may well realize very quickly that a rotating baseball can curve, he is also quite aware that a compact spheroid projectile of high mass density hurled toward him at one hundred plus miles per hour (mach .15) by a pitcher hell bent on getting him "out" is fully capable of inflicting immeasurable pain upon his body.

This keen awareness of risk potential, instinctive in toolies, is somehow lacking in many artsy-craftsies (most noticeably in boxers). This awareness, of course, only accounts for why toolies do not excel in "contact" sports or other sports that involve projectiles, swinging fists, high elevations, or sharp hooks. However, sports having these characteristics include 98.73 percent of all recreational activities known to mankind.

Another characteristic of all toolies is their impulse to shun attention. Thus, although competent to compete in many athletic endeavors, it is not within a toolie's basic nature to want to run around wearing bright-colored tight pants in front of thousands of screaming, intoxicated fans, even less so if the event is played outdoors where it is 35 degrees Fahrenheit (495 degrees Rankine), windy, rainy, and is played on a muddy field.

This is not to say that the only reasons toolies fail to become legendary sports figures is that they're too low-keyed. But given a choice between hitting a game-winning home run in the bottom of the ninth inning, or simply taking four balls and walking to first base, most toolies would seriously consider the merits of the second option.

TOOLIES

CHOOSING A SPORT
Toolies will usually only participate in those sports which offer at least some opportunity for success. The probability of being successful at a sport can be significantly increased by choosing the "right" sport. For toolies, the requisite characteristics of the right sport are:

1) *It must be possible to play alone.* This is an essential characteristic as it eliminates such unnecessary burdens as defenses, competitor ridicule, and honest scorekeeping.

2) *The determination of a win or a loss should be arbitrary,* and ideally the possibility of an actual loss should be almost nonexistent. Clearly, compliance with requisite 1) (no competition or honest scorekeeping) significantly decreases the chance of a loss.

3) *Participation in the sport should not require the wearing of ostentatious clothing.* A toolie's idea of ostentatious clothing is any clothing that is not equally suited to be worn while attending a board meeting or while fixing the next-door neighbor's lawnmower.

GOLF—THE RIGHT SPORT
Of the several sports which fill all the three requisites of the right sport, golf is the sport in which toolies most often participate.

TOOLIES

There are many aspects of golf which are attractive to toolies. It can be played alone. It rarely draws an audience. Everyone dresses as if he came to the course directly from the drafting office. Of particular interest is that golfers rarely fall down (never get pushed down!) and don't get dirty. Golf has a built-in and mandatory success program in that "success" is actually guaranteed by getting the ball in the hole at *every* hole before moving to the next—eighteen built-in successes. (Suppose a batter in baseball *had* to stay at the plate until he got a hit!)

Scorekeeping in golf is one of its most attractive features. It cannot be stated on face whether, for example, a score of eighty-five in golf is a better or worse score than, say, a ninety scored elsewhere and on a different day. Sure, there's always the wind and the rain and the breakdown of ozone molecules in the upper atmosphere which can be used to justify a high score. But what if it's a beautiful day, or you used those excuses yesterday? No problem. Congress long ago passed a federal law mandating that no two golf courses in the world can be made alike. This law was enacted specifically to ensure adequate protection against the possibility of a bad score in golf.

Even with this great equalizer, an honest score in golf is about as easy to find as a fisherman who underestimates the size of his catch. And for the faint of heart, "winter rules"—a sort of legalized cheating—is universally used by toolie duffers year 'round to ensure meaningless scorekeeping for the right sport.

Tool Rules

THE RIGORS OF attorneys and policemen notwithstanding, toolies rely more on laws and rules to govern their day to day activities than any other segment of the population. Toolies continuously make reference to the Laws of Conservation of Energy and the various laws of gravitation and motion. There's L'hopital's Rule, Pythagorus' Theorem, and Pascal's Principle.

In addition to these well known Laws of Nature, toolies are also governed by a separate system of laws, rules, postulates, principles, and maxims which provide them with guidelines on how to conduct themselves in the real world—and what to expect from those who don't.

Artsy-craftsies often make reference to *their* "Murphy's Law" (If anything can go wrong, it will), or *their* "Peter's Principle" (a worker rises in a hierarchy to the level of his incompetence).

But really, although faithfully depicting the artsy-craftsies' world, such laws are of very little practical value. And how could a sappy expression like "A rose by any other name would smell just as sweet" possibly compare with the straight-talking, no-nonsense, and practical first two laws of civil engineering:

"Sewage runs downhill," and "Payday is on Friday."

Pretty much says it all, doesn't it?

The following is a listing of some of the most widely used Toolie Rules:

FIRST LAW OF EXPERT ADVICE—Don't ask a barber if you need a haircut.

FUNDAMENTAL LAW OF COMPUTER SCIENCE—A computer makes as many mistakes in two seconds as ten working men make in twenty years.

FIRST LAW OF RESEARCH AND DESIGN—No matter what stage of completion one reaches in an R & D project, the cost of the remainder of the project remains the same.

FIRST LAW OF CONICAL SECTIONS—Never, never play leap-frog with a unicorn.

FIRST LAW OF NON-RECIPROCAL EXPECTATION—Negative expectation yields negative results.

SECOND LAW OF NON-RECIPROCAL EXPECTATION—Positive expectation yields negative results.

FIRST PRINCIPLE OF TECHNOLOGICAL BREAKTHROUGHS—Do not believe in miracles; count on them.

DRAFTSMAN'S FIRST LAW OF OBSERVATION—When draftsmen appear to be thinking deep thoughts, they probably are thinking about lunch.

LAW OF GOVERNMENT SPECIFICATIONS—An elephant is a mouse built to government specifications.

MOUSE BUILT TO GOVERNMENT SPECIFICATIONS

TOOLIES

FIRST LAW OF ENGINEERING CONTRACTS—The more sure you are that you're going to get it, the less sure you are that you're going to want it.

SECOND LAW OF EXPERT ADVICE—Free advice is worth what you pay for it.

FIRST LAW OF TONGUE HOLDING—Do not insult the mother alligator until after you have crossed the river.

FIRST LAW OF AERODYNAMICS—Never fly on the airline of the country from which you are departing.

SECOND LAW OF RESEARCH & DESIGN—You can't expect to hit the jackpot if you don't put a few nickels in the machine. (Flip Wilson)

FIRST LAW OF FORGIVENESS—Forgive your enemies, but never forget their names. (John Kennedy)

FIRST LAW OF TOOLIE EDUCATION—By the time we've learned all the rules, we're too old to play the game.

THE PATENT PRINCIPLE—He alone discovers who proves. (Simon de Laplace)

FIRST LAW OF DIMINISHING TIME—By spending 10 times as much money, you can cut the time of an engineering project in half. Once.

SECOND DESIGN MAXIM—Everything is equally difficult, designing a new paper clip or a guided missile.

FIRST LAW OF EFFICIENCY—Things that are done illegally are done most efficiently.

SECOND LAW OF DIMINISHING TIME—A professional toolie wasting time loses money for his firm 20 times faster than he earns it.

SECOND LAW OF ENGINEERING CONTRACTS—When the purchaser who doesn't know the difference between good technology and garbage orders good technology, he will always get garbage.

THIRD RULE OF SCIENTIFIC INVESTIGATION—When we eliminate the impossible, whatever remains, however improbable, is the truth. (Sherlock Holmes)

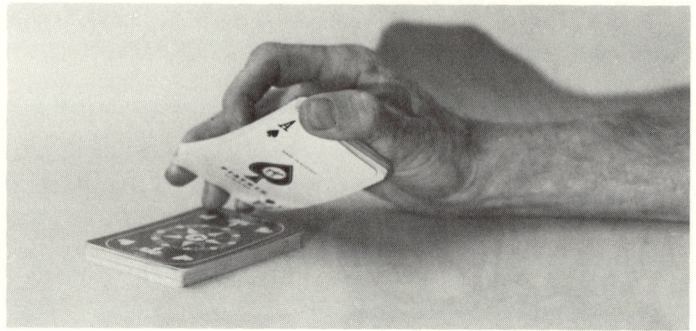
1ST LAW OF RANDOM DISTRIBUTION—Trust all men. But cut the cards.

FIRST LAW OF RANDOM DISTRIBUTION—Trust all men. But cut the cards.

FIRST RULE OF RULES—Young men know the rules, but old men know the exceptions. (Oliver Wendell Holmes)

THIRD LAW OF EXPERT ADVICE—An expert is a person who can tell you more about something than you really care to know.

NUMBERS

One often hears about (other) people who are "good with children." Or perhaps you've seen ladies' men who have reputations for being "good with women." Or maybe you know a sales person who is "good with people her own age."

Well, in describing toolies, the consensus reputation is that they are, if anything, "good with numbers." As in "I hear they're good with numbers, but I wouldn't want my sister to marry one."

Scientific Notation

Are toolies really *that* good with numbers? Well, yes and no.

There is startling evidence suggesting that much of toolies' competency with numbers is based on an illusion, albeit a rather impressive one.

One reason toolies appear to be so familiar with numbers is because they are. Your average toolie actually knows (in the biblical sense) about twenty to thirty numbers. But they know them all very well.

TOOLIES

On the other hand, your basic artsy-craftsy tries to deal with hundreds, even thousands of numbers. How can anyone be intimately familiar with thousands of anything? Quite frankly, the artsy-craftsy brain just isn't quite up to it.

Toolies, you see, only rarely deal with numbers that are bigger than ten or smaller than one. By use of the suitably impressive-sounding "scientific notation," numbers too large to be counted on your fingers are rarely encountered.

For example, the number of grains of sand in a bucket is simply two times ten to the sixth power. The distance in miles the moon is from the earth is said to be two times ten to the fifth power. The number of cubic centimeters in an engine may be two times ten to the second power. And so on.

It was only a short time ago that artsy-craftsies started figuring out what the toolies were up to, what with counting on their fingers and all. But, just when toolies worldwide were about to be exposed, the President's Advisory Commission on Mathematics and Numerical Manipulations published its landmark paper "Big Words for Easy Arithmetic" in which words such as "exponential," "mantissa," and the universally-dreaded "logarithm" became permanently associated with use of such toolie tricks. The pervasive effects of this monumental paper are evident even today as few people other than toolies even attempt to use scientific notation.

Math Studies

Another hidden aspect of this illusion that they are so good with numbers is that the more toolies study math the *less* they actually use those numbers.

Numbers start retreating from toolies' daily usage at about the time they first encounter algebra. This is when the ever-so-popular "X" first appears.

"X" is soon joined by "Y" and "Z," as numbers quickly begin to recede from the picture.

These three "variables" are soon joined by "variable constants" (we're starting to lose it here) "a," "b," and "c."

Next is geometry and trigonometry where not only are operations such as adding and dividing replaced by more mysterious "secants" and "cotangents," but it is also here that "alpha (α)," "beta(β)," "pi (π)," and who-knows-what-all other kinds of prehistoric scratchings replace and all but eliminate the use of numbers.

Numbers become nearly completely foreign by this time, though vague references to such things as "radicals" and (it's true) "imaginary numbers" still show up every once in a while.

Finally toolies become entrenched in the great quagmire that is pompously called The Calculus (which is not to be confused with "a calculus" or "her calculae" or "their calculi" or "Oh! Calcutta").

After several years of The Calculus, a toolie does well to even recognize a number, much less do anything with it. Ask a toolie well into his third year of studies of The Calculus how to determine the appropriate amount to tip a waitress, and the dazed response will sound something like, "Integrate the partial derivative of the inverse cotangent reciprocal by the exponential factorial function of the extrapolated series parameter from gamma prime to the copositive hyperbolic root mean log, as the alpha hexadecimal ordinate of the binary series approaches the Laplace polydecinominal regression of pi times infinity squared. Or two bucks. Whichever is higher."

NUMERIC INTERPRETATION— Understanding Artsy-Craftsy Speech

ALMOST EXACTLY $2.00

Recognizing numbers is only half (.50) of the problem. In a world where artsy-craftsies outnumber toolies (in rough terms) by way-too-much to not-enough, it is usually more difficult to determine *what* quantity is being referred to than it is to determine *how* to use it.

TOOLIES

At first glance most numbers seem to be pretty specifically defined. "Two," you might naively presume, simply means 2, 1 + 1, one pair, one sixth of a dozen, or the positive square root of four. In actuality, it is only toolies who regularly accept such narrow definitions of numbers, while artsy-craftsies attribute a much more liberal meaning to those same numbers (as they do for everything else, for that matter).

As an example, suppose you ask a toolie and an artsy-crafty how much money they have in their pockets, and each replies that he has two dollars. Do they both have the same amount of money? Not likely.

What the toolie response means is that he has exactly two dollars and zero cents.

What the artsy-craftsy response means is that 1) he does have some money, 2) it may be in his pocket (but it also may be in his car), and 3) it's probably more than $1.75, but not likely as much as $3.00.

Or suppose a toolie and an artsy-craftsy each have a length of rope. The toolie says his rope is "about 115 feet long." The artsy-craftsy says his rope is "exactly one hundred feet long." Which rope is longer? Hard to say.

What the toolie's statement means is, "My rope is precisely 115.000 feet long when measured at sea level, with 50 percent relative humidity when ambient temperature is 70 degrees Fahrenheit (22 degrees Celsius) and the barometric pressure equals 29.84 inches of mercury. But since these clouds are moving in and because of its consequential drop in atmospheric pressure, I wouldn't bet my personal computer that it is still precisely 115.000 feet long."

What the artsy-craftsy meant is, "My rope is probably somewhere between 75 and 125 feet long."

Or suppose a toolie and an artsy-craftsy each say that they have "a ton" of homework to turn in on Monday. You're catching on. Obviously they don't have the same amount of homework.

What the toolie is saying is, 1) this looks like an unusually light weekend and, 2) that if he uses a one-half ton pickup truck to carry all his homework in on Monday, the truck will probably structurally fail.

What the artsy-craftsy is saying is that he's gonna be a little late for the Friday night party.

TOOLIES

NUMERICAL CONVERSION RULES AND FACTORS

Fortunately, modern science has discovered a reliable method which now enables toolies, perhaps like yourself, to accurately interpret almost any artsy-craftsy numerical expression. By applying the following two rules and referring to the handy conversion charts, any artsy-craftsy numerical phrase can be easily cross-referenced with its real meaning.

Making these conversions will not reduce your frustration in the check-out line when the artsy-craftsy in front of you escorts enough groceries through the ten items-or-less express lane to feed a small army. Nor will it eliminate your frustration when the driver in front of you is shocked into discovering that the toll booth marked "25 Cents—EXACT CHANGE ONLY" really means "25 Cents—EXACT CHANGE ONLY." But making these conversions may let you get frustrated much more efficiently.

1. Rule of Significant Figures

When spoken by an artsy-craftsy, any number, regardless of its size or its number of digits, has only one "Significant Figure" (and that one is only marginally significant).

EXAMPLE: When spoken by an artsy-craftsy the numbers 2,543 2,999, and 2,000 each have one Significant Figure (2) and all mean the same thing, namely:

$$2^{+1.2}_{-.4} \text{ Thousand} = 2{,}000 ^{+1200}_{-400}$$

or somewhere between 1600 and 3200.

2. Rule of Compounds

When two or more modifiers (see conversion charts) are used together by an artsy-craftsy, their values are multiplied.

EXAMPLE: If an artsy-craftsy tells you that he is absolutely certain that there are precisely almost exactly a half dozen apples in a bag, what he means is:

TOOLIES

Half   Dozen   Precise   Exact   Almost

$\frac{1}{2} \times 12^{+1}_{-2} \times .75 \times .50 \times 1.5 = \frac{9}{16}$

$\phantom{\frac{1}{2}} \times \phantom{12^{+1}_{-2}} \times .75 \times .50 \times 1.5 = 1\frac{1}{8}$

$= 6^{+9/16}_{-1\frac{1}{8}} = 4\frac{7}{8}$ to $6\frac{9}{16}$

You can therefore be 90 to 99 percent ("absolutely") confident that there are between 4-7/8 and 6-9/16 apples. Whether or not they're in the bag is anyone's guess.

Artsy-Craftsy Conversion Table

Artsy-Craftsy Number	Means
1	$1^{+1.1}_{-.3}$
2	$2^{+1.2}_{-.4}$
3	$3^{+1.3}_{-.5}$
4	$4^{+1.4}_{-.6}$
5	$5^{+1.5}_{-.7}$
6	$6^{+1.6}_{-.8}$
7	$7^{+1.7}_{-.9}$
8	$8^{+1.8}_{-1.00}$
9	$9^{+1.9}_{-1.1}$

Example: "3" means $3^{+1.3}_{-.5}$, or anywhere between 2.5 and 4.3.

Modifiers Conversion Chart

Artsy-Craftsy Expression	Means Multiply Tolerance By
Exactly	½
Precisely	¾
Almost	1½
About	2

Level of Confidence Conversion Chart

Artsy-Craftsy Expression	Level of Confidence
Think (Same as "Guess")	0-10%
Know (Same as "Pretty Sure")	10-60%
Sure	60-80%
Positive	80-90%
Absolutely	90-99%

(*Note:* There is no expression whatsoever that means that there is a 100 percent probability that the artsy-craftsy is making an accurate statement.)

TOOLIES

ARTSY-CRAFTSY EXPRESSION	MEANS	REMARKS
NO, NONE, NOT ANY	anything less than few; not enough; not many	As in, "I won't be able to go sailing with you all day Wednesday *and* Thursday—I just have NO free time."
HALF	as modifier, ½; otherwise, anything less than whole.	For example, a box of cookies missing one cookie is said to be HALF empty.
SINGLE	1.000	Along with "PAIR," the only artsy-craftsy numerical expressions having identical toolie values.
PAIR	2.000	Misleadingly simple. A PAIR of socks never means anything but exactly two socks. The subtle difference is that for artsy-craftsies it will be a *matching* pair.
COUPLE	2^{+2}_{-1}	A COUPLE means anything from 1 to 4, and they need not match. For example, toolies wear a COUPLE socks.
FEW	3^{+4}_{-2} (except as applies to time, in which case: 3^{+400}_{-2})	As in, "Hi, I'd like to take just a FEW minutes to discuss with you our very attractive Professionals' Home-Office-Auto-Health-and-Life insurance plan which offers many benefits to persons such as yourself who are...can I call you "Steve"?...who are in a business environment, Steve, not unlike yours, in which the comprehen-

TOOLIES

		sive needs for your fiscal security, Steve, are..."
DOZEN	12^{+1}_{-2}	As in, "We had a DOZEN, but half are gone, so now we only have a few."
TON	4-8 times enough; also, more than 1,000	Has no relationship to weight. As in, "I've got a TON of homework," or "It's a TON of miles from the car to the beach."
MILLION	anything more than 10	As in, "Oh, I've eaten there a MILLION times."
ZILLION	incomprehensibly large	As in, "There must be a ZILLION sesame seeds on this bun."
MEGA-	prefix: big, a lot, or extremely	As in, "He's a MEGA-star, now it costs MEGA-bucks to see him in concert."
MILE	anything long, far	As in, "Hank Aaron could hit a baseball a mile."
110%	90-95%	As in, "I give 110% every day in practice and 110% in every game, but I'm *REALLY* going to play hard tonight since this one is for the championship."

CHAPTER 10

The Metric System— Who Cares?

FOR OVER TWO generations now, American school children have been taught (warned) that the whole country is on the verge to "converting to the metric system." Not only, we have been informed, is this widespread conversion inevitable, but it is imminent. Rarely has anyone ever predicted total conversion to the metric system as being more than two years away. This unrealistic projection has been suggested now for over twenty-five years. The best estimates available today suggest that this conversion is still about two years away.

Surely there must be some reason why an event of such importance has for so long been so near yet so far away. A little historical perspective is of assistance in understanding this development.

THE ENGLISH SYSTEM

The English system of units (feet, pounds, gallons, etc), which is what most Americans who walk upright use, was developed over centuries in many different countries, most of which dropped it a long time ago.

TOOLIES

The reason it took hundreds of years to develop was simply because all types of measurements weren't needed at the same time. Whenever a new type of measurement was needed, whomever happened to be a king at the time would choose some part of his anatomy (or some other similarly arbitrary word) to stand for the new type of measurement.

At the same time, the number of units making up this new measurement would be chosen to be unlike any other standard, thereby avoiding any possible confusion (or so it was thought). This arbitrary nature of the English system is at the root of all that the Prometricites find wrong with the system.

For example, a foot was arbitrarily chosen to be the standard measurement of length. Not your foot, not my foot, nor probably anyone's foot that you know. But one exactly twelve "inches" long. At the time, twelve seemed like a nice number and it wasn't being used for anything else. (The more probable graduation of five or ten per foot would have undoubtedly degraded into being called "toes," a situation wisely avoided from the outset by those in charge of such things.)

When longer distances became popular, similarly arbitrary standards were chosen. A "yard" was chosen to be three feet long. Although it may be argued that as many as one in ten thousand people (twenty thousand feet) will have a twelve-inch-long foot, a recent government-funded survey by a group of anthropologists with nothing better to do came across not one person who had three feet.

When even longer distances were needed, one of the most blatantly arbitrary standards was accepted when it was decided that the new measurement, the "mile," would be exactly—are you ready for this?—5,280 feet long. Now, *that's* a number that definitely wasn't being used for anything else. The English system is filled with such strange and arbitrary units.

So, although the English system is well intended, it is, admittedly, STUPID.

PROMETRICITES

Even though toolies had known the English system was stupid for years, they kept their mouths shut (as they are prone to do) and went

TOOLIES

on about their business. It was only in the last quarter century that a group of artsy-craftsies discovered what the toolies had known all along and decided it was time for a change. Reciting the "everyone-else-is-doing-it, so-it-must-be-OK" rhetoric for which many artsy-craftsies have become known, the metric movement officially got underway in America.

"Everything's done with tens," the prometricites would say. Adding, subtracting, multiplying, cooking, hanging wall paper, walking the dog—everything. And everyone knows how much easier it is to multiply by 10 than by 5,280. So with such simplistic ideas of the metric system, Americans began awaiting the inevitable conversion, which, naturally, shouldn't take but about two years at the most.

As often happens when artsy-craftsies start fiddling in inherently toolie matters*, many problems arose. Things weren't as simple as it was promised. Although efficient and accurate, the metric system somehow seemed too cold, too exact, even un-American. Unlike the English system which took centuries to develop, the metric system was totally conceived, organized, and documented in an hour and a half. Who cares, people began to question, if an answer can be easily reached if no one knows what the answer means? And what's an "erg" anyway?

On the other hand, although the English system is admittedly arbitrary, cumbersome, and, yes, stupid, it is ours. (Sure, nobody else wanted it. But now it's ours.)

There's something warm and personal about making measurements in feet and cups. And even if they are cumbersome to deal with, one gets at least some feeling for both the magnitude and nature of what is being measured when the units are in "tablespoonsful," "feet," "candle power," or "horse power." Ask a two-year-old how big a foot is and he'll not likely be off by more than about, say, a half foot. Ask the same kid how big a millimeter is and he'll probably miss by at least several hundred millimeters. Ask his parents the same

---

* All matters, as it turns out, are inherently toolie matters.

question and they'll probably be even further off.

The toolies, upon whom the prometricites based their initial hopes, have probably turned out to be the movement's own worst enemy. This is due primarily to the prometricites' serious lack of understanding of toolies in two important areas—The Law of Inertia and Pocket Calculators.

Law of Inertia—If you're wrong, stay wrong.

The single most important scientific principle understood by all toolies is that of inertia. Although quantified by Sir Isaac Newton only 150 years ago, inertia has been a time-honored principle of toolieism for several centuries. In short, this principle states that in nature all things will stay as they are until upset by an unbalanced force that acts to mess up the existing situation. (This, the well-coached toolie will be quick to point out, is not his own, but God's law.)

Toolies, as you no doubt are aware, call upon this most important of all laws almost daily. (In texts, toolies call this Newton's First Law of Motion.) In addition to the millions (metric equivalent: 2.54 x millions) of other things this law explains, it also shows why if it weren't for certain unbalanced forces (prometricites), God would personally prefer us to maintain use of the English system.

Pocket Calculators

The second area of toolieism greatly underestimated by the prometricites was manifested in their promoting of the "math is much easier using the metric system" line of reasoning. Once toolies had been made aware of how difficult everything had been using the English system, they had two alternatives to choose between—either change the system or make it easier.

TOOLIES

The first option, change, has already been shown to be, at best, non-preferred.

So, once the decision was made to make the use of the English system easier, it was only (according to best estimates) about twenty-three days until the pocket computer was developed. With the pocket calculator, it became just as easy to multiply 5,280 times 5,280 as to add ten plus ten, if not easier. No longer were any arithmetic problems really difficult, at least to toolies. This miscalculation on the part of the prometricites was a blow that set back the metric conversion movement just about two years.

JEE SUBSEE—THE GREAT ENIGMA

As it turns out, the most convincing argument for abandoning the English system of units in favor of the metric system is one generally unheard of outside of toolie circles; but very well known by toolies.*

Unbeknownst to artsy-craftsies, there is a single number which for some reason is called "jee subsee" (abbreviated g_c), that by itself has caused total confusion among toolies for centuries, has been the sole cause of untold thousands of missed questions on toolie exams, and has even caused many toolies to unintentionally lapse into use of the metric system on many occasions.

Toolies are usually introduced to jee subsee in their introductory physics or mechanics classes. To their horror, that introduction is not to be their last encounter with jee subsee, and in fact, it will seem like jee subsee keeps popping up in every class from then on. Exactly what is it? And why aren't any of these people smiling?

The basic problem (for which no one has been willing to accept the blame) is, simply stated, that a "pound" is not necessarily a "pound"...always. Sometimes. But not always.

When is a Pound Not a Pound?

You see, many years ago it was initially decided that sometimes "pound" would stand for weight. (As in, "This book weighs one

---

* In many states, familiarity with the term "jee subsee" is alone sufficient proof of identification as a toolie.

$$g_c = \frac{385.9 \; lb_m \text{ - in}}{lb_f \text{ - sec}^2}$$

pound.") Then a particularly unimaginative person decided that sometimes "pound" would stand for mass. (As in, "This book has a mass of one pound.") In retrospect, the old system of having a king name each unit after a different part of his anatomy would have been far less confusing. (Maybe "This book has a mass of one knee-cap," or "This book weighs twenty-four ear lobes" would have been better.)

What aggravates this already confusing situation is that "mass" and "weight" are fairly similar concepts to begin with, and to call them both the same name is ludicrous. This is kind of like having non-identical twin daughters and naming them both Mary.

That's where jee subsee comes in. Jee subsee is (supposedly) used to change one type of "pound" into the other type of "pound." Unfortunately, the two types of "pounds" are inherently different, so you can't really do that. On the other hand, sometimes the two "pounds" are already the same, which they can't really be, in which case to employ jee subsee to change one "pound" into the other will only make them more different. So no matter what you do, you will do the wrong thing. And as a rule, whatever you do will make you incorrect by a factor of jee subsee. This, as you might suspect, is not the thing that accurate calculations or good grades are made of!

To make matters worse, almost no standard handbooks ever tell you which "pound" they are talking about. When using charts from such handbooks, it is suggested that for each item you first multiply by jee subsee, then divide by jee subsee, then if neither of these approaches gives you the answer that you are looking for, find another book with the data given in the metric system (which, mercifully, doesn't have this problem).

Steps have been taken in recent years to resolve the problems caused by the ambiguous use of the word "pound" in engineering measurements. A special Bureau of Standards (B.S.) task force that did not include even one king supposedly relieved this immense confusion when it selected the word "slug" (indicating perhaps the mood they were in) to take the place of one of these "pounds." Unfortunately, no one to date knows which one.

CHAPTER 11

Endangered Species

A VARIETY OF toolie tools, once abundant in this country, are now faced with the very real possibility of extinction. Attempts to explain the trend towards fewer and fewer toolie tools have thus far been quite inadequate.

Some say it's swamp gas, while others blame it on acid rain or excessive use of fluron in deodorant sprays. And although some suggest that it is only a passing condition associated with increased sunspot activity, the diminishing number of toolie tools is still of immense concern to most toolies.

The interdependence between man and his environment cannot be overlooked and we can ill-afford to continue to squander our resources. It is of grave concern for the future of toolies that, if it is true that without toolies there can be no tools, then it also holds that without tools there can be no toolies.

Grim reminders of other professions whose tools became extinct suggest an ominous future should steps not be taken immediately to preserve toolie tools. For example, it was only shortly after the disappearance of the buggy whip that there were suddenly—that's right—no more buggies and no more buggy drivers.

Coincidence? Perhaps.

Sunspots? Perhaps.

But it would clearly be imprudent for toolies to follow a similar course in view of these observations.

CLIPBOARD—Don't leave home without it.

THE CLIPBOARD

The single most important toolie tool used today, and one of the few not in immediate danger of total extinction, is the clipboard. Only the mechanical pencil is more widely used by toolies than the clipboard. And let's face it, anybody can own a mechanical pencil these days.

Concisely stated, the clipboard represents the epitome of toolieism. A manifestation of the fundamentals of classic engineering design, the clipboard is a low cost, highly reliable, high quality, unflashy, very functional piece of equipment. The life span of the standard clipboard is 427 years. The clipboard's design is perhaps the ultimate in "appropriate technology"*

Opening Doors

But the real value of the clipboard as an engineering classic can only be gauged accurately by considering its functionality. That is, how well does the clipboard accomplish the job for which it was originally

---

*Admittedly, this is an artsy-craftsy expression. As you know, technology is always appropriate.

designed—opening doors?!

On this account, the clipboard receives its highest marks. For, as all toolies find out sooner or later, there are virtually no doors which cannot be opened by a good clipboard in the hands of a skilled toolie. By properly displaying this internationally recognized pass, not only can one gain admittance to any building or security area, one also receives immediate and full cooperation from the area's occupants.

The correct method of entering an unauthorized area is by holding a clipboard in the left hand, about chest-high. The clipboard should never be down to the side, as it may appear as though you are in some need of guidance which could lead to well-intended, but extremely embarrassing, questions from the area's occupants.

Head positioning is also very important. Your head should be slightly tilted with your eyes focused somewhere between straight ahead and directly down at the clipboard. For best results you should use the same blank stare that served you so well in high-school when your English teacher scanned the room for someone to recite Mark Antony's eulogy from *Julius Ceasar*.

Until you have perfected your own clipboard entry style, you should carry a mechanical pencil in your right hand. And, for better effect, cock you elbow so that you appear ready to either 1) check off whether what you see passes the strict requirements that might be written on your clipboard, or 2) write down the names of anyone who dares question your entrance.

An extremely controversial question is whether or not you should wear a hard hat to enhance your door-opening possibilities. The correct answer is no—not if you are already carrying your clipboard. And, besides, you probably look goofy in a hard hat.

SLIDE RULE

This, the quintessential toolie tool for nearly one thousand years, is now all but extinct.

Conservationists speak of a time when engineers were engineers. When it took someone special to calculate cube roots, natural logs, and y to the x power. Now they say you can't tell the players from the fans. Today anyone can perform these operations on hand-

TOOLIES

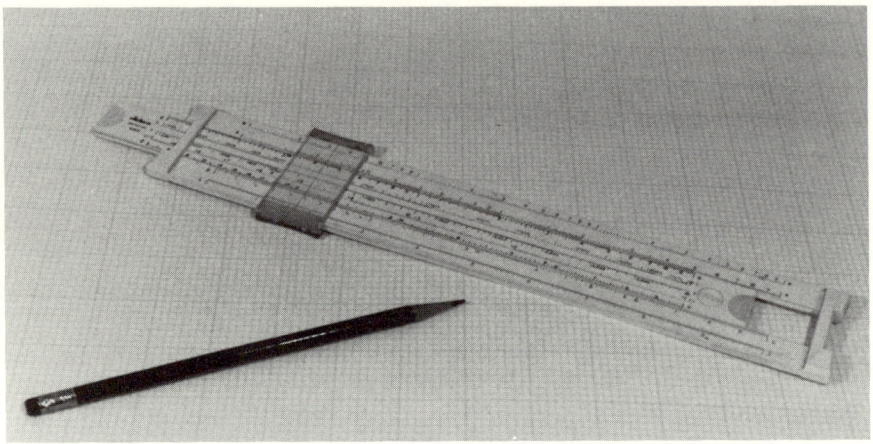

held calculators, even if they have no idea what they're doing.

Some say it's strictly a case of evolution moving ahead while others suggest a calculated conspiracy of extermination propogated by manufacturers of pocket calculators. In any event, the time when any master toolie could be recognized by his leather-cased finely-crafted "slip stick" hanging proudly from his belt is now just a memory.

MATH TABLES

Like the proverbial slide rule, math tables have also significantly reduced in number (so to speak) since the evolution of the pocket calculator.

Under the genus "math tables" (Listei Arithmetus) there are several subspecies which are either already technically extinct or are approaching extinction (i.e. the limit as subspecie approaches zero). The closest of these to extinction include trig tables, squares, cubes, square roots, cube roots, and common logarithm tables.

Periodically, sightings are reported of one or two people per year actually looking up the square root of a number in a math table, but such sightings are becoming quite rare. Other math tables, including the subspecies "definite integrals," "LaPlace transforms," and "Fourier series," are about as popular today as they ever were. But, you guessed it, they never were too popular in the first place.

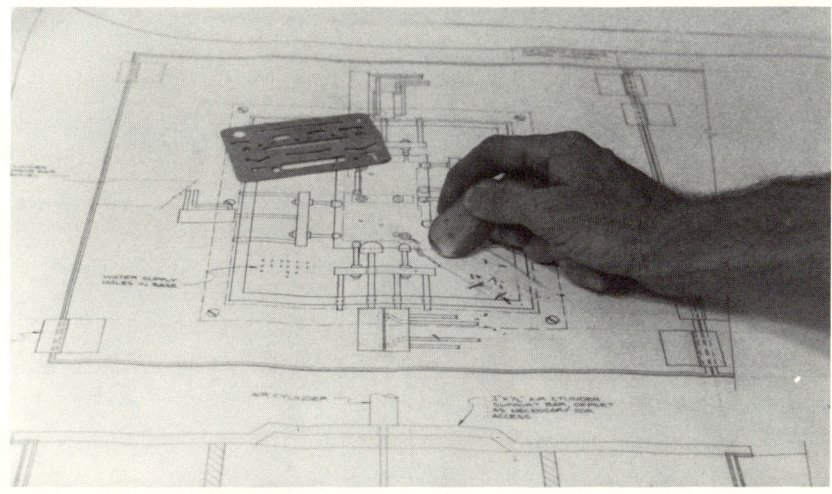

MANUAL ERASER

Manual erasers are presently "penciled in" on the list of threatened species, though not quite so rare as those tools classified as "extinct."

Researchers inform us that manual erasers are dwindling in number due primarily to 1) natural attrition, 2) electric erasers, 3) word processors, and 4) CAD-CAM.

With the advent of the electric eraser several years ago, manual erasers quickly became scarce around drafting departments. With the recent widespread acceptance of word processors, CAD/CAM, and other computer aids, it has become possible to erase whole pages electronically, cleanly, quickly, and easily.

Many eraserologists believe, however, that because of the encouraging news that the frequency of mistakes has been dramatically increasing during the last several years, erasers of all kinds are starting to make a strong comeback.

T-SQUARE

The Toolie-Square (abbreviated, "T-Square") has been steadily diminishing in numbers throughout the past forty years. Replaced by drafting machines, parallel straight edges, and the ominous CAD/CAM, the T-Square was once a prized possession of the skilled toolie. Although periodic T-Square sightings are reported, such sightings are usually on engineering office walls or in the hands of painters, and are rarely used for their designed purpose.

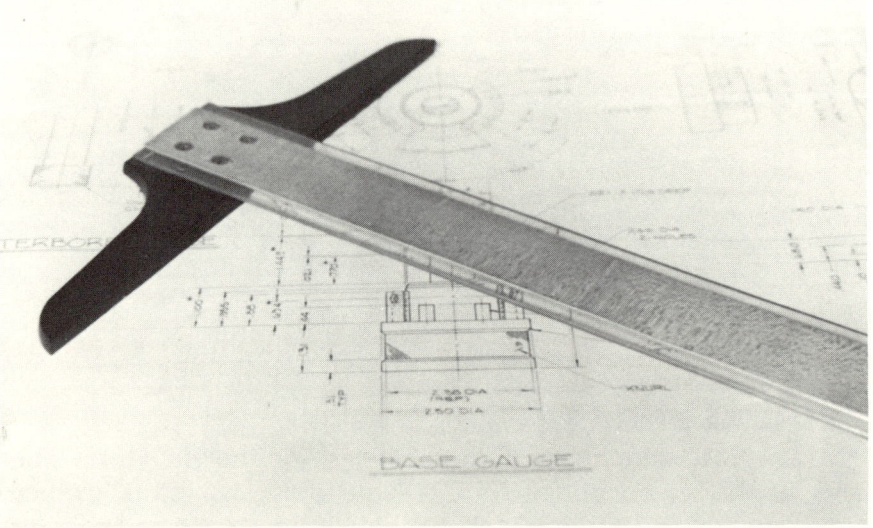

RULING PENS

Nearly extinct, but hardly missed at all is the double-nibbed ink pen.

For centuries, ink precariously held only by its own surface tension leaked out from these pens—all over drawings. Untold millions of hours of lost time resulted from the damage done by the India ink that uncontrollably spilled from these pens.

TOOLIES

Recent improvements—primarily the needle point pens and ink cartridges—quickly sent these pens into extinction.

Today, remains of these pens are primarily found only in drafting sets that were assembled by manufacturers who got stuck with an enormous inventory of these pens several years ago and have yet to determine any other way to get rid of them.

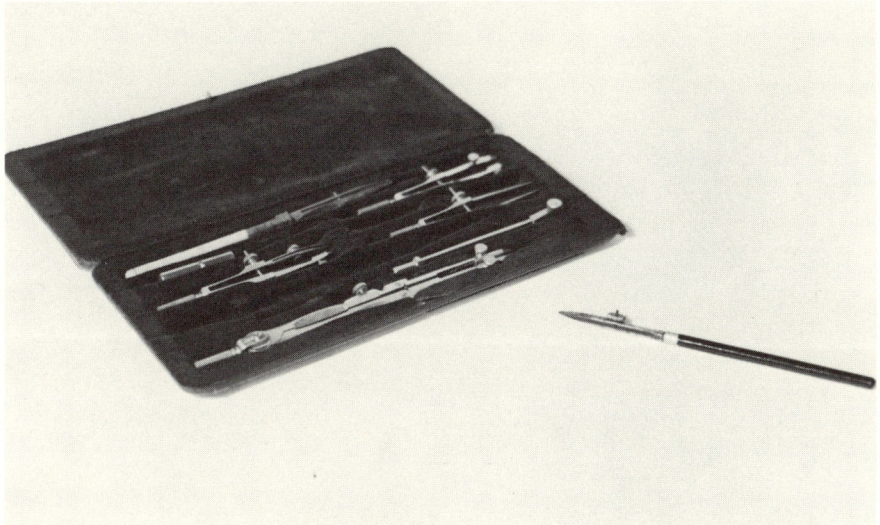

THREATENED SPECIES
Drafting Linen (Tracing Cloth)
Wooden Pencils
Wooden Engineer Scales
Bubble-Sight Transits
Adding Machines
IBM Cards (Apparently too many were folded, spindled, or mutilated)

CHAPTER 12

They Said It Couldn't Be Done

FEW TECHNOLOGICAL ACHIEVEMENTS have been accomplished without being preceded by the requisite barrage of skepticism from the reputedly "open minded" masses who seem always to be available to tell the toolie that "it'll never work."

Most of us are so used to such well-intended but off-based conclusions from artsy-craftsies that such remarks do not warrant much attention, and formal denunciation is utterly inappropriate. This is a kind of "attitude partial credit," reserved generally only for artsy-craftsies.

Occasionally, though, toolies have been known to make a few miscalculations themselves, and accordingly, deserve to be severely chastised for such blunders. Surely they would want it that way.

The following is only a sample of some of those miscalculations, some made by artsy-craftsies and some by toolies:

TOOLIES

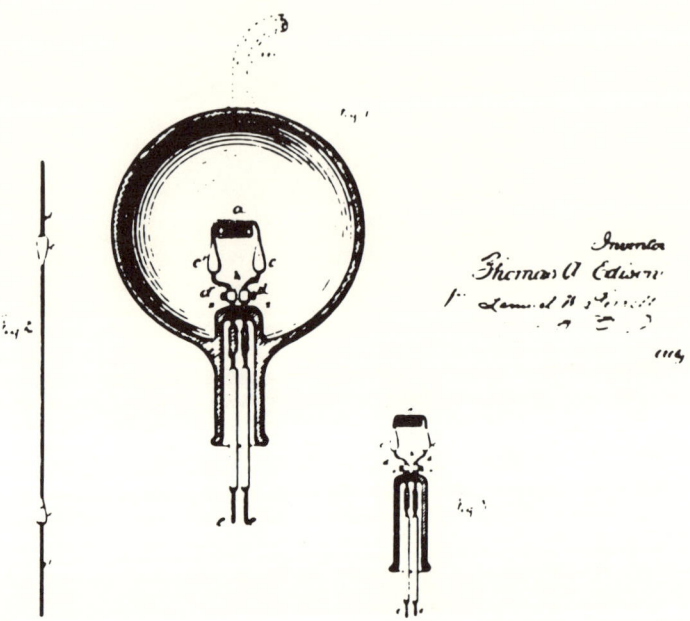

In 1889 the patent office was almost closed because it was believed that everything worth inventing had already been invented.

"The speculation...is interesting, but the impossiblity of ever doing it is so certain that it is not practically useful."
—Editor of *Popular Astronomy* to
Robert Goddard, who had proposed
nuclear energy, 1902

"Flight by machines heavier than air is unpractical and insignificant, if not utterly impossible."
—Simon Newcomb, eminent astronomer,
eighteen months before the Wright brothers'
first flight

"Fooling around with alternating current is just a waste of time."
—Thomas Edison

"Rail travel at high speed is not possible, because passengers, unable to breathe, would die of asphyxia."
—Dr. Dionysus Lardner (1793-1859), professor
of natural philosophy and astronomy at
University College, London

"No large steamship could ever cross the Atlantic."
—Dr. Lardner (ibid)

"We hope that Professor Langley will not put his substantial greatness as a scientist in further peril by continuing to waste his time and the money involved in further airship experiments. Life is too short..."
—*The New York Times,* editorial, 1903

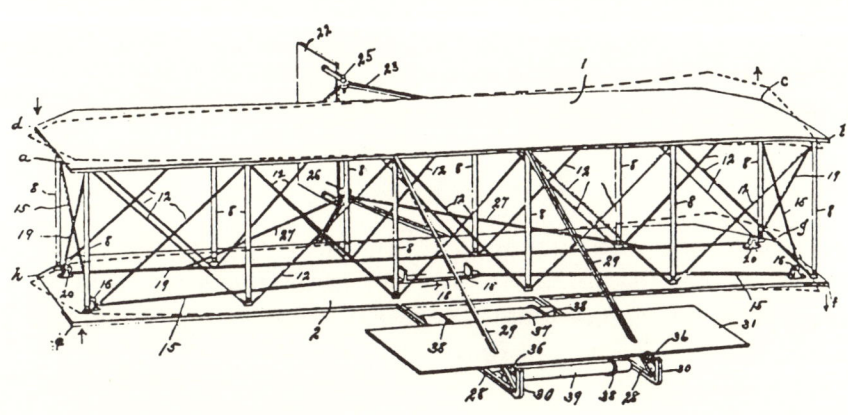

"...Physically impossible to withstand a speed much over 400 miles per hour..."
—Dr. Starr Truscott, aeronautical engineer
for National Advisory Committee for
Aeronautics, 1929

TOOLIES

"Young man, you can be grateful that my invention is not for sale, for it would undoubtedly ruin you. It can be exploited for a certain time, but apart from that it has no commercial value whatsoever."
—August Lumiere, commenting on
moving pictures, 1935

"To fix fleeting reflections is not only impossible as has been shown by thorough-going German research, but to wish do so so is blasphemy."
—(Leipzig) *City Advertiser* regarding
announcements of Daguerre's discoveries
regarding arrival of photography

"It will never be possible to synchronize the voice with the pictures.... There will never be speaking pictures."
—D. W. Griffith, 1924

"Americans require a restful quiet in the moving picture theatre, and for them talking...on screen destroys the illusion. Devices for projecting the film actor's speech can be prefaced, but the idea is not practical."
—Thomas Edison, 1926

American family hasn't time for it. Therefore, the showmen are convinced that for this reason, if no other, television will never be a serious competitor of broadcasting."
—*The New York Times* March, 1939

"I cannot conceive of any use that the fleet will ever have for aircraft...aviation is just a lot of noise."
—Admiral Charles Benson,
CNO after World War I

Einstein's parents feared he was retarded and a teacher of his told him he would never amount to anything.

TOOLIES

"...even considering the improvements possible... the gas turbine could hardly be considered a feasible application to airplanes because of the difficulty in complying with the stringent weight requirements..."
—U. S. National Academy of Sciences, 1946

"Because of its widespread availability, its enormous destructive capabilities, and its ability to bypass geographic boundaries, the invention of this device will effectively bring an end to war forever as its use will make it impossible for either side of an armed conflict to win."
—Prevailing wisdom regarding dynamite, circa 1000
—Prevailing wisdom regarding gatling gun, circa 1850
—Prevailing wisdom regarding the airplane, circa 1920
—Prevailing wisdom regarding the atomic bomb, circa 1980

"As far as sinking a ship with a bomb is concerned, you just can't do it."
—Rear Admiral Clark Woodward, 1939

"It couldn't be done."
—They

FAMOUS WEALTHY ENGINEERS

The following is a comprehensive list of names, telephone numbers, addresses, and dates of registration of all practicing Professional Engineers who are included among the one thousand wealthiest people in America:

(end of list)

TOOLIE HALL OF FAME

> "When a true genius appears in the world, you may know him by this sign, that the dunces are all in a confederacy against him."
> —Frank Lloyd Wright

In addition to minor hurdles such as media condemnation or imprisonment or lack of funding or excommunication or widespread public harassment or lack of government support or even the possibility of execution, toolies historically have even been confronted with many *serious* obstacles to achieving personal recognition. The greatest of these obstacles is the toolies' inherent aversion to accept publicity—to say nothing of actually going out and promoting it.

History has also shown us that of the toolies who do achieve widespread acclaim, it is often only their dabbling in secondary endeavors that brings them their recognition.

For example, two of the United States' first three presidents were toolies at heart.* It was only after George Washington, that well-known surveyor from Mount Vernon, took time off from his true toolie interests that he led the colonies to military victory in the Revolutionary War and became president and father of his country.

And don't forget Thomas Jefferson. After authoring the Declaration of Independence and attending to a few other diversions, Jefferson became the first administrator of the U. S. Patent Office, then designed (we're talking complete architectural plans here) the University of Virginia, the Virginia State Capitol building, his home Monticello, and various other buildings, while at the same time

---

* More recently during this century, presidents Hoover and Carter have brought toolieism to the White House.

Herbert Hoover, a Stanford-educated engineer you will probably recall, had the typically toolie-style luck of seeing the stock market crash shortly after he put both his feet into the White House.

Jimmy Carter ("Jimmy," for heaven's sakes), a U. S. Naval Academy-educated nuclear engineer, spent four years in Washington trying to be just another one of the guys (having fireside chats, wearing cardigan sweaters, carrying his own suitcase, selling the presidential yacht, etc.). In the true tradition of toolie understatement, Jimmy surely secured his place in history next to the likes of Millard Fillmore (who?) on the list of soon-to-be-forgotten ex-Commanders-in-Chief.

TOOLIES

inventing numerous innovations for use around his farm and maintaining extensive and detailed scientific logs of meteorological, astronomical, and agricultural occurances.

THOMAS JEFFERSON—First administrator of the United States Patent Office

But did either Washington or Jefferson become widely known because of their toolie endeavors? Nooooo.

To be sure, thousands of the world's most important technological breakthroughs were born in the minds of toolies whose names are now all but unknown. And I don't just mean the little stuff, but the really important inventions—like the slicing, dicing Veg-a-matic and the automatic-powered bed that, with a simple push of a button, can fold itself into any one of over a hundred certifiably uncomfortable positions. And don't forget that wonderful buzzer that relentlessly throbs when you get into your car if you dare be so imprudent as to forget to lock your door, buckle your seat belt, close your tailgate, check the battery, brush your teeth, and put out the cat—all in the name of A Better Way of Life for all mankind.

And did we ever stop to thank them? You should be ashamed of yourself.

There are, however, a few toolies who in spite of overwhelming odds (read: artsy-craftsies) are widely recognized for their immense contributions to mankind. The following members of the Toolie Hall of Fame are presented to pay tribute not just to those who are listed, but to all the other toolies to whom these represent role models.

Leonardo da Vinci (1452-1519), Italian; Greatest engineer/architect/scientist of the Renaissance; an accomplished draftsman; also reputed to have dabbled in painting and sculpting; a toolie ahead of his time, having invented the kite, the glider, and the helicopter nearly two hundred years before Sir Isaac Newton even discovered gravity.

Newton, Sir Isaac (1642-1727), English mathematician/engineer/scientist; recognized as one of the greatest scientists of all time; best known for formulating the Universal Laws of Gravitation and Motion, which form the basis of nearly all of classical physics; most importantly, discovered fundamental laws of inertia which even today dictate the basis for all conservative toolie behavior; also developed The Calculus.

ALBERT EINSTEIN

Einstein, Albert (1879-1955), German physicist; laid foundation for all modern physics; his General Theory of Relativity brought about fundamental changes in the theories of the universe; formulated mathematical relationship between matter, energy, and time; also set a standard of non-ostentatious grooming technique for a generation of aspiring scientists.

God (Beginning of time-   ), (photograph not available), all time greatest architect/engineer; multi-disciplined; best works include solar system, autumn and spring, snowy egret, puppy dogs; greatest design setbacks include Duckbilled Platypus and Sahara Forest.

Edison, Thomas A. (1847-1931), American inventor; secured patents for 1,033 inventions, including vote recorder, stock ticker, electric pen, carbon transmitter, phonograph, and carbon and tungsten filament electric light bulbs; not considered a profound scientist (formal school limited to only three months and was never any good at math); genius at embodying scientific principles in practical devices; unkempt appearance gave support to claim that you can dress toolies up, but they always look like toolies; said to have slept only three hours per night, possibly because the light switch wasn't invented until several years after his invention of the electric light. (This, however, has not been confirmed.)

THOMAS A. EDISON

Brothers, Wright (Wilbur, 1867-1912; Orville, 1871-1948), American inventors; erstwhile bicycle shop operators; fathers of powered flight; invented first fully successful glider with three-axis flight control and invented first controlled flight, powered airplane; although efforts led to one of the most significant technological achievements in the history of mankind, their landmark first flight at Kitty Hawk, North Carolina, in classic toolie fashion, was reported in only one newspaper; five years after the fact, leading national papers covered their first powered flight; received so little interest in their invention from the United States government that most of their subsequent development was carried out in France where their work was more appreciated.

TOOLIES

WRIGHT BROTHER

WRIGHT BROTHER

Razafat, Abdul (circa 900 B.C.), Egyptian architect/engineer/ camel driver; took advantage of "networking;" had friends in high places; member, Giza (Egypt) Community Development Council; Chief Project Engineer/Consultant on Pyramid Project, Phases I and II; prepared detailed plans and specifications for successful construction of pyramid monoliths; expertise in design of foundations, tunnels, and vaults; early proponent of "symmetry in architecture;" name obscured by early detractors who said "Raz's follies" were overdesigned; nevertheless, his structures were invariably completed *way* under budget (with the help of slave labor) and have clearly withstood the test of time.

Archimedes (287-212 B. C), Greek mathematician/physicist/ inventor; famous for his work in geometry, physics, mechanics, and hydrostatics; world's greatest toolie until Leonardo; inventor of Archimedes' (who else's?) Screw; upon discovering the laws regarding the buoyancy of floating objects while bathing, is said to have rushed from his bath naked shouting, "Eureka!;" in recognition of this singular and extraordinary deviation from the normal demeanor of toolie decorum, this outrageous episode has henceforth been known as "Archimedes' Principle."

TOOLIES

GALILEO GALILEI

Galilei, Galileo (1564-1642), Italian astronomer, physicist; laid foundations to modern experimental science; discovered mechanics of pendulum; his development of the pendulum clock significantly advanced cause of scientific investigation; also contributed to invention of microscope, telescope, thermometer, barometer, and hydrostatic balance; imprisoned after the Artsy-Craftsy Inquisition for suggesting that the earth revolves around the sun; extensive studies of the sun with telescope led directly to the discovery of sunspots as well as his own blindness; all-time greatest contribution to science made at Leaning Tower of Pisa when, after suggesting (of all things) that every object falls toward the ground at the same speed, he was then forced to invent the "coefficient," which is now widely used in absolutely every aspect of toolie life.

Afterword

IF YOU'VE READ this entire book and you are still not convinced that toolies are significantly different from the average person on the street, or perhaps you started at the back of the book (which is what toolies are prone to do) and have not yet read about these distinctions, consider this: the toolie brain is crammed full of facts that most people, including toolies themselves, have no need and no desire whatsoever to remember. But no matter how hard you try to purge your mind of this worthless data, your toolie brain will simply not let them go.

For example, a toolie couldn't forget that sixteen is the atomic weight of an oxygen molecule, or four squared, or that it is the base of the hexadecimal numbering system even if his/her hypoteneuse depended on it. "So what?" you say.

Below is a list of other numbers which exemplify this non-purgeable toolie mind clutter. You will immediately recognize the "significance" of nearly every one. Some are missing their descriptive units of measurement and some are actually missing whole digits, but you don't care. You still know what they refer to.

You may even think that most are so obvious that everyone recognizes these numbers. Not so! Show this list to any artsy-craftsy and you will then realize unequivocably that you are not one of them!

TOOLIE MIND CLUTTER

What Does This Number Mean To You?	Remarks
.707	one-half the square root of two; sine and cosine of 45 degrees; RMS value of sine wave having an amplitude of 1; number of horsepower in one BTU/sec
(?).1416	pi with the "3" left off—even some artsy-craftsies recognize 3.1416 as π
3×10^8 (or 3×10^{10})	speed of light, meters/second (cm/sec)
62.4	density of water, lb/cubic foot
30-60-90	the three angles of one of your most popular triangles
57.29	degrees per radian
2.54	centimeters per inch
9/5 (?) + 32	conversion factor, centigrade to Fahrenheit (or is it Fahrenheit to centigrade?)
1, 2, $\sqrt{3}$	relative lengths of sides of a 30-60-90 triangle
550 (or 33,000)	ft-lb/sec per horse power, (or ft-lb/min per hp) (This is the worst kind of toolie mind clutter. You knew that it had *something* to do with horsepower, but you didn't remember exactly what.)

TOOLIES

2.718	e, the base for natural logarithms
1.732	square root of 3
273	degrees Kelvin, equivalent to zero degrees C and 32 degrees Fahrenheit
39.37	inches per meter
14.7	psi, 1 atmosphere; atmospheric pressure at sea level
6.023×10^{23}	Avogadro's number (This is another serious waste of your brain cells that you probably didn't even know were being wasted. Sure, you recognize this is Avogadro's number, but you really don't know what it means, and you certainly couldn't have recited it if you had been asked its value.)
13.6	specific gravity of mercury. (O.K., this might have been a tough one.)
.125	decimal equivalent of ⅛ (Did you hear yourself? "This one is so easy it *must* refer to something else.")
186,000	speed of light, miles/sec
32.174	acceleration due to gravity, feet/second squared

Q.E.D.
(Quod erat demonstrandum)

Index

A
Activists, political   33
Athletes, brainless   24
Arch, Gateway   42
Archimedes   120

B
Breasts, buxom women's   43
Brothers, Dr. Joyce   4
Brothers Wright   4, 112, 119, 120
Bulb, light   119

C
Cats, lighting fire to   78
Clerk, grocery   69, 70
Congress   83

D
Daughters, twin   102
Doors, opening   104, 105
Doughnut, chocolate   68
Dumpster, garbage   77

E
Edison, Thomas   112, 114, 119
Egg drop contest   18
Einstein, Albert   114, 118
Entropy   19, 38
Eraser, electric   61, 107
Execution   116

F
Five year programs   14, 27
Flight, impossibility of   112, 113

G
Galilei, Galileo   121
Garbage men   62
Gas, Swamp   103
God   118
Granola bars   61
Ground, feet on   52

H
Harassment, public   116
Hierarchy, toolie   67, 68
Hot tub   70

I
Imaginary Numbers   19, 90
Imbeeay   11, 12, 70

J
Jeesubsee   19, 101, 102
Jefferson, Thomas   32, 116, 117

K
Kings, anatomies of   98

L
Leonardo DaVinci   60, 118
Low Bidders   42, 70

M
Matchbook covers, advertising in   22
Metric System   97–101
Mind clutter   Afterword

N
Napkins, writing on   46
Newton, Sir Isaac   57, 118
North Pole   28

O
Open book tests   6, 7
Ostentacious clothing   82

P
Pet animals, doing kinky thing to   78
Plaid, inability to wear   37, 43
Prometricites   98
Prunes   37

Q
Quality, unimportance of   71

R
Razafat, Abdul   120
Resume amplification   73
Rock singers   4
Rules, slide   105, 106
Rules, tool   85–88

S
Schroedinger wave equation   19
Scratchings, prehistoric   90
Sewage   86
Sex   5
Shakespeare, William   8, 9
Surveyors   4, 63

T
Tan, sun   63
Technology, appropriate   104
Train drivers   2, 3
Triangle, 3-4-5   14, Afterword
Triange, 30-60-90   14, Afterword

U
Unicorn, leapfrog with   86
Unions, labor   66

V
Vacuum, absolute   51, 54
Vertical Transportation Consultants   4

W
Widget Thingamabob, Framastatic   59